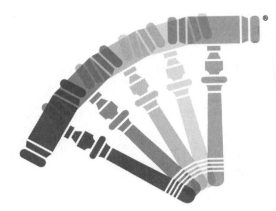

Casenote™ *Legal Briefs*

EVIDENCE

Keyed to
Mueller and Kirkpatrick's
Evidence under the Rules
Fifth Edition

ASPEN
PUBLISHERS

1185 Avenue of the Americas, New York, NY 10036
www.aspenpublishers.com

This publication is designed to provide accurate and authoritative information in regard to the subject matter covered. It is sold with the understanding that the publisher is not engaged in rendering legal, accounting, or other professional services. If legal advice or other expert assistance is required, the services of a competent professional person should be sought.

— From a *Declaration of Principles* adopted jointly by a Committee of the American Bar Association and a Committee of Publishers and Associates

About Aspen Publishers

Aspen Publishers, headquartered in New York City, is a leading information provider for attorneys, business professionals, and law students. Written by preeminent authorities, our products consist of analytical and practical information covering both U.S. and international topics. We publish in the full range of formats, including updated manuals, books, periodicals, CDs, and online products.

Our proprietary content is complemented by 2,500 legal databases, containing over 11 million documents, available through our Loislaw division. Aspen Publishers also offers a wide range of topical legal and business databases linked to Loislaw's primary material. Our mission is to provide accurate, timely, and authoritative content in easily accessible formats, supported by unmatched customer care.

To order any Aspen Publishers title, go to *www.aspenpublishers.com* or call 1-800-638-8437.

For more information on Loislaw products, go to *www.loislaw.com* or call 1-800-364-2512.

For Customer Care issues, e-mail CustomerCare@aspenpublishers.com; call 1-800-234-1660; or fax 1-800-901-9075.

Aspen Publishers
A Wolters Kluwer Company

FORMAT FOR THE CASENOTE LEGAL BRIEF

PARTY ID: Quick identification of the relationship between the parties.

NATURE OF CASE: This section identifies the form of action (e.g., breach of contract, negligence, battery), the type of proceeding (e.g., demurrer, appeal from trial court's jury instructions) or the relief sought (e.g., damages, injunction, criminal sanctions).

FACT SUMMARY: This is included to refresh the student's memory and can be used as a quick reminder of the facts.

CONCISE RULE OF LAW: Summarizes the general principle of law that the case illustrates. It may be used for instant recall of the court's holding and for classroom discussion or home review.

FACTS: This section contains all relevant facts of the case, including the contentions of the parties and the lower court holdings. It is written in a logical order to give the student a clear understanding of the case. The plaintiff and defendant are identified by their proper names throughout and are always labeled with a (P) or (D).

ISSUE: The issue is a concise question that brings out the essence of the opinion as it relates to the section of the casebook in which the case appears. Both substantive and procedural issues are included if relevant to the decision.

HOLDING AND DECISION: This section offers a clear and in-depth discussion of the rule of the case and the court's rationale. It is written in easy-to-understand language and answers the issue(s) presented by applying the law to the facts of the case. When relevant, it includes a thorough discussion of the exceptions to the case as listed by the court, any major cites to other cases on point, and the names of the judges who wrote the decisions.

CONCURRENCE / DISSENT: All concurrences and dissents are briefed whenever they are included by the casebook editor.

EDITOR'S ANALYSIS: This last paragraph gives the student a broad understanding of where the case "fits in" with other cases in the section of the book and with the entire course. It is a hornbook-style discussion indicating whether the case is a majority or minority opinion and comparing the principal case with other cases in the casebook. It may also provide analysis from restatements, uniform codes, and law review articles. The editor's analysis will prove to be invaluable to classroom discussion.

QUICKNOTES: Conveniently defines legal terms found in the case and summarizes the nature of any statutes, codes, or rules referred to in the text.

PALSGRAF v. LONG ISLAND R.R. CO.
Injured bystander (P) v. Railroad company (D)
N.Y. Ct. App., 248 N.Y. 339, 162 N.E. 99 (1928).

NATURE OF CASE: Appeal from judgment affirming verdict for plaintiff seeking damages for personal injury.

FACT SUMMARY: Helen Palsgraf (P) was injured on R.R.'s (D) train platform when R.R.'s (D) guard helped a passenger aboard a moving train, causing his package to fall on the tracks. The package contained fireworks which exploded, creating a shock that tipped a scale onto Palsgraf (P).

CONCISE RULE OF LAW: The risk reasonably to be perceived defines the duty to be obeyed.

FACTS: Helen Palsgraf (P) purchased a ticket to Rockaway Beach from R.R. (D) and was waiting on the train platform. As she waited, two men ran to catch a train that was pulling out from the platform. The first man jumped aboard, but the second man, who appeared as if he might fall, was helped aboard by the guard on the train who had kept the door open so they could jump aboard. A guard on the platform also helped by pushing him onto the train. The man was carrying a package wrapped in newspaper. In the process, the man dropped his package, which fell on the tracks. The package contained fireworks and exploded. The shock of the explosion was apparently of great enough strength to tip over some scales at the other end of the platform, which fell on Palsgraf (P) and injured her. A jury awarded her damages, and R.R. (D) appealed.

ISSUE: Does the risk reasonably to be perceived define the duty to be obeyed?

HOLDING AND DECISION: (Cardozo, C.J.) Yes. The risk reasonably to be perceived defines the duty to be obeyed. If there is no foreseeable hazard to the injured party as the result of a seemingly innocent act, the act does not become a tort because it happened to be a wrong as to another. If the wrong was not willful, the plaintiff must show that the act as to her had such great and apparent possibilities of danger as to entitle her to protection. Negligence in the abstract is not enough upon which to base liability. Negligence is a relative concept, evolving out of the common law doctrine of trespass on the case. To establish liability, the defendant must owe a legal duty of reasonable care to the injured party. A cause of action in tort will lie where harm, though unintended, could have been averted or avoided by observance of such a duty. The scope of the duty is limited by the range of danger that a reasonable person could foresee. In this case, there was nothing to suggest from the appearance of the parcel or otherwise that the parcel contained fireworks. The guard could not reasonably have had any warning of a threat to Palsgraf (P), and R.R. (D) therefore cannot be held liable. Judgment is reversed in favor of R.R. (D).

DISSENT: (Andrews, J.) The concept that there is no negligence unless R.R. (D) owes a legal duty to take care as to Palsgraf (P) herself is too narrow. Everyone owes to the world at large the duty of refraining from those acts that may unreasonably threaten the safety of others. If the guard's action was negligent as to those nearby, it was also negligent as to those outside what might be termed the "danger zone." For Palsgraf (P) to recover, R.R.'s (D) negligence must have been the proximate cause of her injury, a question of fact for the jury.

EDITOR'S ANALYSIS: The majority defined the limit of the defendant's liability in terms of the danger that a reasonable person in defendant's situation would have perceived. The dissent argued that the limitation should not be placed on liability, but rather on damages. Judge Andrews suggested that only injuries that would not have happened but for R.R.'s (D) negligence should be compensable. Both the majority and dissent recognized the policy-driven need to limit liability for negligent acts, seeking, in the words of Judge Andrews, to define a framework "that will be practical and in keeping with the general understanding of mankind." The Restatement (Second) of Torts has accepted Judge Cardozo's view.

QUICKNOTES
FORESEEABILITY – The reasonable anticipation that damage is a likely result from certain acts or omissions.
NEGLIGENCE - Failure to exercise that degree of care which a person of ordinary prudence would exercise under similar circumstances.
PROXIMATE CAUSE – Something which in natural and continuous sequence, unbroken by any new intervening cause, produces an event, and without which the injury would not have occurred.

NOTE TO STUDENTS

Aspen Publishers is proud to offer *Casenote Legal Briefs*—continuing thirty years of publishing America's best-selling legal briefs.

Casenote Legal Briefs are designed to help you save time when briefing assigned cases. Organized under convenient headings, they show you how to abstract the basic facts and holdings from the text of the actual opinions handed down by the courts. Used as part of a rigorous study regime, they can help you spend more time analyzing and critiquing points of law than on copying out bits and pieces of judicial opinions into your notebook or outline.

Casenote Legal Briefs should never be used as a substitute for assigned casebook readings. They work best when read as a follow-up to reviewing the underlying opinions themselves. Students who try to avoid reading and digesting the judicial opinions in their casebooks or on-line sources will end up shortchanging themselves in the long run. The ability to absorb, critique, and restate the dynamic and complex elements of case law decisions is crucial to your success in law school and beyond. It cannot be developed vicariously.

Casenote Legal Briefs represent but one of the many offerings in Aspen's Study Aid Timeline, which includes:

- Casenotes *Legal Briefs*
- Emanuel *Outlines*
- *Examples & Explanations* Series
- *Introduction to Law* Series
- Emanuel *Law in a Flash* Flashcards
- Emanuel *CrunchTime* Series

Each of these series is designed to provide you with easy-to-understand explanations of complex points of law. Each volume offers guidance on the principles of legal analysis and, consulted regularly, will hone your ability to spot relevant issues. We have titles that will help you prepare for class, prepare for your exams, and enhance your general comprehension of the law along the way.

To find out more about Aspen Study Aid publications, visit us on-line at www.aspenpublishers.com or e-mail us at legaledu@aspenpubl.com. We'll be happy to assist you.

Free access to Briefs on-line!

Download the cases you want in your notes or outlines using the full cut-and-paste feature accompanying our on-line briefs. Please fill out this form for full access to this useful feature. No photocopies of this form will be accepted.

① **Name:** _____ **Phone: (____)** _____

   Address: _____ **Apt.:** _____

   City: _____ **State:** _____ **ZIP Code:** _____

   Law School: _____ **Year (circle one):**   1st   2nd   3rd

② **Cut out the UPC found on the lower left-hand corner of the back cover of this book. Staple the UPC inside this box. Only the original UPC from the book cover will be accepted. (No photocopies or store stickers are allowed.)**

> **Attach UPC inside this box.**

③ **E-mail:** _____ **(Print LEGIBLY or you may not get access!)**

④ **Title (course subject) of this book** _____

⑤ **Used with which casebook (provide author's name):** _____

⑥ **Mail the completed form to:**   Aspen Publishers, Inc.
                                     Legal Education Division
                                       Casenote On-line Access
                                       675 Massachusetts Ave., 11th floor
                                       Cambridge, MA 02139

I understand that on-line access is granted solely to the purchaser of this book for the academic year in which it was purchased. Any other usage is not authorized and will result in immediate termination of access. Sharing of codes is strictly prohibited.

_____

Signature

Upon receipt of this completed form, you will be e-mailed codes so that you may access the Briefs for this Casenote Legal Brief. On-line Briefs may not be available for all titles. For a full list of available titles please check www.aspenpublishers.com/casenotes.

HOW TO BRIEF A CASE

A. DECIDE ON A FORMAT AND STICK TO IT

Structure is essential to a good brief. It enables you to arrange systematically the related parts that are scattered throughout most cases, thus making manageable and understandable what might otherwise seem to be an endless and unfathomable sea of information. There are, of course, an unlimited number of formats that can be utilized. However, it is best to find one that suits your needs and stick to it. Consistency breeds both efficiency and the security that when called upon you will know where to look in your brief for the information you are asked to give.

Any format, as long as it presents the essential elements of a case in an organized fashion, can be used. Experience, however, has led *Casenotes* to develop and utilize the following format because of its logical flow and universal applicability.

NATURE OF CASE: This is a brief statement of the legal character and procedural status of the case (e.g., "Appeal of a burglary conviction").

There are many different alternatives open to a litigant dissatisfied with a court ruling. The key to determining which one has been used is to discover *who is asking this court for what.*

This first entry in the brief should be kept as *short as possible.* The student should use the court's terminology if the student understands it. But since jurisdictions vary as to the titles of pleadings, the best entry is the one that apprises the student of who wants what in this proceeding, not the one that sounds most like the court's language.

CONCISE RULE OF LAW: A statement of the general principle of law that the case illustrates (e.g., "An acceptance that varies any term of the offer is considered a rejection and counteroffer").

Determining the rule of law of a case is a procedure similar to determining the issue of the case. Avoid being fooled by red herrings; there may be a few rules of law mentioned in the case excerpt, but usually only one is *the* rule with which the casebook editor is concerned. The techniques used to locate the issue, described below, may also be utilized to find the rule of law. Generally, your best guide is simply the chapter heading. It is a clue to the point the casebook editor seeks to make and should be kept in mind when reading every case in the respective section.

FACTS: A synopsis of only the essential facts of the case, i.e., those bearing upon or leading up to the issue.

The facts entry should be a short statement of the events and transactions that led one party to initiate legal proceedings against another in the first place. While some cases conveniently state the salient facts at the beginning of the decision, in other instances they will have to be culled from hiding places throughout the text, even from concurring and dissenting opinions. Some of the "facts" will often be in dispute and should be so noted. Conflicting evidence may be briefly pointed up. "Hard" facts must be included. Both must be *relevant* in order to be listed in the facts entry. It is impossible to tell what is relevant until the entire case is read, as the ultimate determination of the rights and liabilities of the parties may turn on something buried deep in the opinion.

The facts entry should never be longer than one to three *short* sentences.

It is often helpful to identify the role played by a party in a given context. For example, in a construction contract case the identification of a party as the "contractor" or "builder" alleviates the need to tell that that party was the one who was supposed to have built the house.

It is always helpful, and a good general practice, to identify the "plaintiff" and the "defendant." This may seem elementary and uncomplicated, but, especially in view of the creative editing practiced by some casebook editors, it is sometimes a difficult or even impossible task. Bear in mind that the *party presently* seeking something from this court may not be the plaintiff, and that sometimes only the cross-claim of a defendant is treated in the excerpt. Confusing or misaligning the parties can ruin your analysis and understanding of the case.

ISSUE: A statement of the general legal question answered by or illustrated in the case. For clarity, the issue is best put in the form of a question capable of a "yes" or "no" answer. In reality, the issue is simply the Concise Rule of Law put in the form of a question (e.g., "May an offer be accepted by performance?").

The major problem presented in discerning what is *the* issue in the case is that an opinion usually purports to raise and answer several questions. However, except for rare cases, only one such question is really the issue in the case. Collateral issues not necessary to the resolution of the matter in controversy are handled by the court by language known as *"obiter dictum"* or merely *"dictum."* While dicta may be included later in the brief, it has no place under the issue heading.

To find the issue, the student again asks *who wants what* and then goes on to ask *why did that party succeed or fail in getting it.* Once this is determined, the "why" should be turned into a question.

The complexity of the issues in the cases will vary, but in all cases a single-sentence question should sum up the issue. *In a few cases,* there will be two, or even more rarely, three issues of equal importance to the resolution of the case. Each should be expressed in a single-sentence question.

Since many issues are resolved by a court in coming to a final disposition of a case, the casebook editor will reproduce the portion of the opinion containing the issue or issues most relevant to the area of law under scrutiny. A noted law professor gave this advice: "Close the book; look at the title on the cover." Chances are, if it is Property, the student need not concern himself with whether, for example, the federal government's treatment of the plaintiff's land really raises a federal question sufficient to support jurisdiction on this ground in federal court.

The same rule applies to chapter headings designating sub-areas within the subjects. They tip the student off as to what the text is designed to teach. The cases are arranged in a casebook to show a progression or development of the law, so that the preceding cases may also help.

It is also most important to remember to *read the notes and questions* at the end of a case to determine what the editors wanted the student to have gleaned from it.

HOLDING AND DECISION: This section should succinctly explain the rationale of the court in arriving at its decision. In capsulizing the "reasoning" of the court, it should always include an application of the general rule or rules of law to the specific facts of the case. Hidden justifications come to light in this entry; the reasons for the state of the law, the public policies, the biases and prejudices, those considerations that influence the justices' thinking and, ultimately, the outcome of the case. At the end, there should be a short indication of the disposition or procedural resolution of the case (e.g., "Decision of the trial court for Mr. Smith (P) reversed").

The foregoing format is designed to help you "digest" the reams of case material with which you will be faced in your law school career. Once mastered by practice, it will place at your fingertips the information the authors of your casebooks have sought to impart to you in case-by-case illustration and analysis.

B. BE AS ECONOMICAL AS POSSIBLE IN BRIEFING CASES

Once armed with a format that encourages succinctness, it is as important to be economical with regard to the time spent on the actual reading of the case as it is to be economical in the writing of the brief itself. This does not mean "skimming" a case. Rather, it means reading the case with an "eye" trained to recognize into which "section" of your brief a particular passage or line fits and having a system for quickly and precisely marking the case so that the passages fitting any one particular part of the brief can be easily identified and brought together in a concise and accurate manner when the brief is actually written.

It is of no use to simply repeat everything in the opinion of the court; the student should only record enough information to trigger his or her recollection of what the court said. Nevertheless, an accurate statement of the "law of the case," i.e., the legal principle applied to the facts, is absolutely essential to class preparation and to learning the law under the case method.

To that end, it is important to develop a "shorthand" that you can use to make margin notations. These notations will tell you at a glance in which section of the brief you will be placing that particular passage or portion of the opinion.

Some students prefer to underline all the salient portions of the opinion (with a pencil or colored underliner marker), making marginal notations as they go along. Others prefer the color-coded method of underlining, utilizing different colors of markers to underline the salient portions of the case, each separate color being used to represent a different section of the brief. For example, blue underlining could be used for passages relating to the concise rule of law, yellow for those relating to the issue, and green for those relating to the holding and decision, etc. While it has its advocates, the color-coded method can be confusing and time-consuming (all that time spent on changing colored markers). Furthermore, it can interfere with the continuity and concentration many students deem essential to the reading of a case for maximum comprehension. In the end, however, it is a matter of personal preference and style. Just remember, whatever method you use, underlining must be used sparingly or its value is lost.

For those who take the marginal notation route, an efficient and easy method is to go along underlining the key portions of the case and placing in the margin alongside them the following "markers" to indicate where a particular passage or line "belongs" in the brief you will write:

N   (NATURE OF CASE)
CR   (CONCISE RULE OF LAW)
I   (ISSUE)
HC   (HOLDING AND DECISION, relates to the CONCISE RULE OF LAW behind the decision)
HR   (HOLDING AND DECISION, gives the RATIONALE or reasoning behind the decision)
HA   (HOLDING AND DECISION, APPLIES the general principle(s) of law to the facts of the case to arrive at the decision)

Remember that a particular passage may well contain information necessary to more than one part of your brief, in which case you simply note that in the margin. If you are using the color-coded underlining method instead of margin notation, simply make asterisks or checks in the margin next to the passage in question in the colors that indicate the additional sections of the brief where it might be utilized.

The economy of utilizing "shorthand" in marking cases for briefing can be maintained in the actual brief writing process itself by utilizing "law student shorthand" within the brief. There are many commonly used words and phrases for which abbreviations can be substituted in your briefs (and in your class notes also). You can develop abbreviations that are personal to you and which will save you a lot of time. A reference list of briefing abbreviations will be found elsewhere in this book.

C. USE BOTH THE BRIEFING PROCESS AND THE BRIEF AS A LEARNING TOOL

Now that you have a format and the tools for briefing cases efficiently, the most important thing is to make the time spent in briefing profitable to you and to make the most advantageous use of the briefs you create. Of course, the briefs are invaluable for classroom reference when you are called upon to explain or analyze a particular case. However, they are also useful in reviewing for exams. A quick glance at the fact summary should bring the case to mind, and a rereading of the concise rule of law should enable you to go over the underlying legal concept in your mind, how it was applied in that particular case, and how it might apply in other factual settings.

As to the value to be derived from engaging in the briefing process itself, there is an immediate benefit that arises from being forced to sift through the essential facts and reasoning from the court's opinion and to succinctly express them in your own words in your brief. The process ensures that you understand the case and the point that it illustrates, and that means you will be ready to absorb further analysis and information brought forth in class. It also ensures you will have something to say when called upon in class. The briefing process helps develop a mental agility for getting to the *gist* of a case and for identifying, expounding on, and applying the legal concepts and issues found there. Of most immediate concern, that is the mental process on which you must rely in taking law school examinations. Of more lasting concern, it is also the mental process upon which a lawyer relies in serving his clients and in making his living.

ABBREVIATIONS FOR BRIEFING

acceptance	acp		offer	O
affirmed	aff		offeree	OE
answer	ans		offeror	OR
assumption of risk	a/r		ordinance	ord
attorney	atty		pain and suffering	p/s
beyond a reasonable doubt	b/r/d		parol evidence	p/e
bona fide purchaser	BFP		plaintiff	P
breach of contract	br/k		prima facie	p/f
cause of action	c/a		probable cause	p/c
common law	c/l		proximate cause	px/c
Constitution	Con		real property	r/p
constitutional	con		reasonable doubt	r/d
contract	K		reasonable man	r/m
contributory negligence	c/n		rebuttable presumption	rb/p
cross	x		remanded	rem
cross-complaint	x/c		res ipsa loquitur	RIL
cross-examination	x/ex		respondeat superior	r/s
cruel and unusual punishment	c/u/p		Restatement	RS
defendant	D		reversed	rev
dismissed	dis		Rule Against Perpetuities	RAP
double jeopardy	d/j		search and seizure	s/s
due process	d/p		search warrant	s/w
equal protection	e/p		self-defense	s/d
equity	eq		specific performance	s/p
evidence	ev		statute of limitations	S/L
exclude	exc		statute of frauds	S/F
exclusionary rule	exc/r		statute	S
felony	f/n		summary judgment	s/j
freedom of speech	f/s		tenancy in common	t/c
good faith	g/f		tenancy at will	t/w
habeas corpus	h/c		tenant	t
hearsay	hr		third party	TP
husband	H		third party beneficiary	TPB
in loco parentis	ILP		transferred intent	TI
injunction	inj		unconscionable	uncon
inter vivos	I/v		unconstitutional	unconst
joint tenancy	j/t		undue influence	u/e
judgment	judgt		Uniform Commercial Code	UCC
jurisdiction	jur		unilateral	uni
last clear chance	LCC		vendee	VE
long-arm statute	LAS		vendor	VR
majority view	maj		versus	v
meeting of minds	MOM		void for vagueness	VFV
minority view	min		weight of the evidence	w/e
Miranda warnings	Mir/w		weight of authority	w/a
Miranda rule	Mir/r		wife	W
negligence	neg		with	w/
notice	ntc		within	w/i
nuisance	nus		without prejudice	w/o/p
obligation	ob		without	w/o
obscene	obs		wrongful death	wr/d

TABLE OF CASES

A

Abel, United States v. 56

B

Bagaric, United States v. 96
Baker v. Elcona Homes Corp. 32
Baker v. State 52
Barber v. Page 34
Betts v. Betts 12
Biggins, United States v. 97
Blake v. State 28
Bourjaily v. United States 23
Bruton v. United States 19

C

Cain v. George 9
Chapple, State v. 3
Check, United States v. 9
Collins, People v. 5
Crawford v. Washington 41

D

Daubert v. Merrell Dow Pharmaceuticals 66
Doe, United States v. 91
Doyle v. Ohio 21
Duffy, United States v. 100

E

Estes, United States v. 89

F

Fowler, United States v. 46

G

Gould, United States v. 79
Grand Jury Investigation 83-2-35 (Durant), *In re,* 86
Griffin v. California 90

H

Harris v. New York 61
Havens, United States v. 63
Hoosier, United States v. 20
Houser v. State 78
Howard-Arias, United States v. 95

I

Idaho v. Wright 42
Iron Shell, United States v. 25

J

Jaffee v. Redmond 87
James Julian, Inc. v. Raytheon Co. 53
Jenkins v. Anderson 62

Johnson, United States v. 94
Jones, United States v. 77

K

Kovel, United States v. 83
Kumho Tire Co., Ltd. V. Carmichael 67

L

Lightly, United States v. 46
Lipscomb, United States v. 58
Lloyd v. American Export Lines, Inc. 35
Luce v. United States 59

M

Mahlandt v. Wild Canid Survival & Research
    Center 22
Manske, United States v. 57
Medical Therapy Sciences, United
    States v. 64
Meredith, People v. 82
Meyers v. United States 101
Moore, State v. 68
Motta, State v. 18
Muller v. Oregon 78
Mutual Life Insurance Co. v. Hillmon 26

N

Norcon v. Kotowski 31
Nuttall v. Reading Co. 24

O

Oates, United States v. 33
Ohio v. Roberts 40
Ohio v. Scott 29
Old Chief v. United States 2
Old Chief v. United States (II) 4

P

Pacelli, United States v. 11
Patterson v. New York 71
Petrocelli v. Gallison 30
Pheaster, United States v. 27
Phelps, State v. 86
Pool, United States v. 97

R

Ricketts v. Delaware 47
Rock v. Arkansas 48

S

Sandstrom v. Montana 72
Singer, United States v. 10

TABLE OF CASES (Continued)

Smith, State v. 15
Suburban Sew 'N Sweep v. Swiss-Bernia 84
Sylvania Electric Products v. Flanagan 102

T

Tanner v. United States 49
Texas Department of Community Affairs v.
    Burdine 70
Tome v. United States 16
Trammel v. United States 88
Tuer v. McDonald 44

U

Ulster, County of, v. Allen 73
Upjohn Co. v. United States 85

V

Virgin Islands, Govt. of, v. Gereau 76

W

Weaver, State v. 39
Webster, United States v. 60
Williamson v. United States 37
Wright v. Doe d. Tatham 8

2

CHAPTER 2*
RELEVANCE

QUICK REFERENCE RULES OF LAW

1. **Relevance and Materiality.** Relevant evidence may be excluded when its risk of unfair prejudice substantially outweighs its probative value, in view of the availability of alternative evidence on the same point. (Old Chief v. United States (I))

2. **Prejudice and Confusion.** Inflammatory evidence should not be admitted if not probative of any contested issue in the case. (State v. Chapple)

3. **Prejudice and Confusion.** In determining whether to admit evidence under the balancing test of Fed. R. Evid. 403, the court must weigh the probative value of the evidence sought to be admitted against the risk of unfair prejudice in light of the entire evidentiary record. (Old Chief v. United States (II))

4. **The Relevance of Probabilistic.** Applications of mathematical techniques in the proof of facts in a criminal case must be critically examined in view of the substantial unfairness to the defendant which may result. (People v. Collins)

*There are no cases in Chapter 1.

OLD CHIEF v. UNITED STATES
Convicted felon (D) v. Government (P)
519 U.S. 172 (1997).

NATURE OF CASE: Appeal from conviction for possession of firearm.

FACT SUMMARY: Old Chief (D) offered to stipulate to a prior felony conviction to avoid admitting the full record of his prior offense when he was charged with violation of a statute prohibiting the possession of firearms.

CONCISE RULE OF LAW: Relevant evidence may be excluded when its risk of unfair prejudice substantially outweighs its probative value, in view of the availability of alternative evidence on the same point.

FACTS: Old Chief (D) was charged with violation of a statute that prohibited the possession of a firearms by anyone convicted of a crime punishable by imprisonment exceeding one year. Old Chief (D) had a previous felony conviction of assault that fell within the purview of the statute. At trial, Old Chief (D) moved to exclude the name and nature of his prior conviction in exchange for a stipulation that he had been convicted of a crime punishable by imprisonment exceeding one year. The trial judge refused Old Chief's (D) stipulation, and the jury convicted him on all counts. Old Chief (D) appealed.

ISSUE: May relevant evidence be excluded when its risk of unfair prejudice substantially outweighs its probative value, in view of the availability of alternative evidence on the same point?

HOLDING AND DECISION: (Souter, J.) Yes. Relevant evidence may be excluded when its risk of unfair prejudice substantially outweighs its probative value judged in the context of the availability of alternative evidence on the same point. Although the prosecution is entitled to prove its case by the evidence of its own choice, this rule has no application where the evidence is not essential in providing a continuous story of its case against the defendant. The proper test is to balance the degrees of probative value and unfair prejudice for the evidence in question and for alternative, relevant evidence. The alternative evidence may be admitted if it carries the same or greater probative value, but a lower risk of unfair prejudice than the evidence in question. Reversed.

EDITOR'S ANALYSIS: The term "unfair prejudice" speaks to the capacity of some concededly relevant evidence to lure the fact finder into declaring guilt on a ground different from proof specific to the offense charged. In other words, a defendant's earlier bad act may be generalized into bad character, thereby raising the odds that he did the act he is charged with. Even worse, some juries might feel justified in practicing "preventive conviction," even if they believe the defendant is momentarily innocent.

QUICKNOTES

PROBATIVE - Tending to establish proof.

RELEVANCE - The admissibility of evidence based on whether it has any tendency to prove or disprove a matter at issue to the case.

NOTES:

STATE v. CHAPPLE

Government (P) v. Convicted murderer (D)

660 P.2d 1208 (Ariz. 1983).

NATURE OF CASE: Appeal of conviction for first-degree murder.

FACT SUMMARY: A trial court admitted inflammatory evidence which was not probative of any contested issue in the case.

CONCISE RULE OF LAW: Inflammatory evidence should not be admitted if not probative of any contested issue in the case.

FACTS: Chapple (D) was charged with first-degree murder in the shooting death of one Varnes. Chapple (D) did not contest the identity of the victim, nor the cause of death. The only matter he contested was his identification by two eyewitnesses. At trial, the State (P) offered various color photographs of the victim's body. The photos were of a gruesome nature. The photos were not probative as to the eyewitness identification issue. The photos were admitted, and Chapple (D) was convicted. He appealed.

ISSUE: Should inflammatory evidence be admitted if not probative of any contested issue in the case?

HOLDING AND DECISION: (Feldman, J.) No. Inflammatory evidence should not be admitted if not probative of any contested issue in the case. When proffered evidence is of an inflammatory nature, the usual rule that all evidence is admissible if relevant is not necessarily followed. Even if a court determines that the evidence is relevant, it must weigh the probative value of the evidence against its prejudicial effect. When the evidence is not probative of any contested issue, its probative value is minimal and it should be excluded. Here, the only issue was identification of the perpetrator and the photographs were not probative of this issue. They should have been excluded. Reversed.

EDITOR'S ANALYSIS: This rule is fairly consistent throughout the various jurisdictions. It is codified in Fed. R. Evid. 403. Even though the trial court was reversed in this instance, much discretion is usually left to the court.

QUICKNOTES

PROBATIVE - Tending to establish proof.

NOTES:

OLD CHIEF v. UNITED STATES (II)
Convicted felon (D) v. Government (P)
519 U.S. 172 (1997).

NATURE OF CASE: Appeal from charge of being a felon in possession of a firearm and assault with a dangerous weapon.

FACT SUMMARY: Old Chief (D) offered to stipulate to a prior felony conviction to avoid admitting the full record of his prior offense when he was charged with violation of a statute prohibiting the possession of firearms.

CONCISE RULE OF LAW: In determining whether to admit evidence under the balancing test of Fed. R. Evid. 403, the court must weigh the probative value of the evidence sought to be admitted against the risk of unfair prejudice in light of the entire evidentiary record.

FACTS: Old Chief (D) was charged with violation of a statute that prohibited the possession of a firearms by anyone convicted of a crime punishable by imprisonment exceeding one year. Old Chief (D) had a previous felony conviction of assault that fell within the purview of the statute. At trial, Old Chief (D) moved to exclude the name and nature of his prior conviction in exchange for a stipulation that he had been convicted of a crime punishable by imprisonment exceeding one year. The trial judge refused Old Chief's (D) stipulation, and the jury convicted him on all counts. Old Chief (D) appealed.

ISSUE: In determining whether to admit evidence under the balancing test of Fed. R. Evid. 403, must the court weigh any probative value the evidence sought to be admitted might have against the risk of unfair prejudice in light of the entire evidentiary record?

HOLDING AND DECISION: (Souter, J.) Yes. In determining whether to admit evidence under the balancing test of Fed. R. Evid. 403, the court must weigh the probative value of the evidence sought to be admitted against the risk of unfair prejudice in light of the entire evidentiary record. In balancing the probative value of the evidence against the risk of unfair prejudice under Fed. R. Evid. 403, there are two possibilities. Either the item of evidence may be considered alone, or it may be considered in context of the totality of the evidentiary record. If an objection is raised, then the court must decide whether the particular item presents a danger of unfair prejudice. If so, the judge must evaluate the degrees of probative value and unfair prejudice for the item or any available substitutes. Where its probative value is substantially outweighed by unfair prejudicial risk, then the item will be disclosed. Under this approach a defendant's Fed. R. Evid. 403 objection offering to concede a point would not prevail over the prosecution's decision to offer evidence of guilt and all the circumstances surrounding the offense. The commentary to Fed. R. Evid. 403 makes it clear that the term "probative value" refers to the consideration of one item of evidence while the term "relevance" involves the comparison of evidentiary alternatives. The comments also state that a party's concession is relevant to the court's discretion to exclude evidence relating to the point conceded. Such decisions are to be made on the bases of expedience and undue prejudice, not relevance. Moreover, the comments state that in making such a ruling the court may consider the availability of alternative means of proof. Evidence of the name or nature of a prior offense normally risks unfair prejudice to the defendant. Here, as in any other case in which a prior conviction is likely to support a conviction on an improper ground, the risk of unfair prejudice outweighed the probative value of the conviction record. The court abused its discretion in admitting the record when an admission was available. Reversed and remanded.

DISSENT: (O'Connor, J.) Here, one is not found guilty of a crime or felony but of "a specified offense." Troubling is the majority's argument that the general principle favoring evidentiary depth has "virtually no application" in this case since a jury is "as likely to be puzzled" by a "missing chapter" relating to a prior felony conviction as it would be by a concession of any other element in the crime.

EDITOR'S ANALYSIS: Note that the Court limits its holding to actions that involve proof that the defendant is a felon. Generally, appellate review of a decision under Fed. R. Evid. 403 requires the defendant to demonstrate the lower court abused its discretion in admitting or not admitting the evidence. This requires a greater showing than mere proof of alternative evidence.

NOTES:

4

PEOPLE v. COLLINS
Government (P) v. Convicted robber (D)
438 P.2d 33 (Cal. 1968).

NATURE OF CASE: Appeal from conviction of second-degree robbery.

FACT SUMMARY: In the People's (P) suit against Collins (D) for second-degree armed robbery, Collins (D) contended that testimony admitted into evidence at trial as to the mathematical probability that Collins (D) committed the crime unduly influenced the jury and infected the case with fatal error.

CONCISE RULE OF LAW: Applications of mathematical techniques in the proof of facts in a criminal case must be critically examined in view of the substantial unfairness to the defendant which may result.

FACTS: In the People's (P) suit against Collins (D) for second-degree robbery, the prosecution experienced some difficulty in establishing the perpetrators of the robbery. In order to bolster the identification of Collins (D) as the perpetrator, the prosecutor called a mathematics instructor from a state college who testified about the mathematical probability that persons who possessed the various characteristics possessed by Collins (D) and his wife, a co-defendant, existed. The witness inferred that there could be but one chance in twelve million that Collins (D) and his wife were innocent and that another equally distinctive couple actually committed the robbery. Collins (D) objected to the witness' testimony on the grounds that it was based on unfounded assumptions. Collins (D) was convicted and appealed on the grounds that the mathematician's testimony infected the case with fatal error.

ISSUE: Must applications of mathematical techniques in the proof of facts in a criminal case be critically examined in view of the substantial unfairness to the defendant which may result?

HOLDING AND DECISION: (Sullivan, J.) Yes. Application of mathematical techniques in the proof of facts in a criminal case must be critically examined in view of the substantial unfairness to the defendant which may result. Here, the prosecution's theory of probability rested on the assumption that the witness called by the People (P) had conclusively established that the guilty couple possessed the precise characteristics relied upon by the prosecution. But no mathematical formula could ever establish beyond a reasonable doubt that the prosecution's witness correctly observed and accurately described the distinctive features which were employed to link the Collinses (D) to the crime. The most a mathematical computation could ever yield would be a measure of the probability that a random couple would possess the distinctive features in question. Reversed.

EDITOR'S ANALYSIS: It appears that the explicit use of theories of probability and statistical inference remains controversial. This is true whether the theories serve either as a basis for the opinions of the experts themselves or as a course of education for jurors in how to think about scientific identification evidence. However, as long as counsel and the experts do not try to place a scientific seal of approval on results not shown to be grounded in science, there is probably room for judicious use of these theories to put identification evidence in perspective.

NOTES:

CHAPTER 3
HEARSAY

QUICK REFERENCE RULES OF LAW

1. **Nonassertive Conduct.** Hearsay statements offered to establish a fact based upon the opinion of the declarant are inadmissible. (Wright v. Doe d. Tatham)

2. **Nonassertive Conduct.** Evidence regarding complaints is not hearsay. (Cain v. George)

3. **Indirect Hearsay.** The hearsay rule cannot be circumvented by framing testimony so as to suggest what an unavailable declarant said. (United States v. Check)

4. **Hearsay and Nonhearsay — Statements with Performative Aspects.** Evidence of conduct not intended as an assertion of fact is not made inadmissible by the hearsay rule. (United States v. Singer)

5. **Using Statements to Prove Matters Assumed.** Testimony regarding statements which imply facts presented to prove their own truth is hearsay. (United States v. Pacelli)

6. **Hearsay — Test your Understanding.** Statements which are relevant whether or not they are true do not implicate the hearsay rule. (Betts v. Betts)

WRIGHT v. DOE d. TATHAM
Steward (D) v. Cousin of deceased (P)
Ct. of Exchequer Chamber, 7 Ad. & E. 313, 112 Eng. Rep. 488 (1837).

NATURE OF CASE: Appeal from order validating a will.

FACT SUMMARY: Tatham (P) contended letters written to the testator Marsden were admissible to prove the mental capacity of Marsden at the time the will was made.

CONCISE RULE OF LAW: Hearsay statements offered to establish a fact based upon the opinion of the declarant are inadmissible.

FACTS: Marsden died testate leaving valuable property to his steward, Wright (D). Tatham (P), Marsden's cousin, sued to invalidate the will, contending Marsden lacked mental capacity to effect a valid will. Wright (D) introduced two letters written by different individuals to Marsden relating to various legal matters. The purpose of these letters was to establish that the writers of the letters considered Marsden legally competent to attend to his own affairs. Based in part upon these letters which were entered into evidence, the will was upheld. Tatham (P) appealed, contending the content of the letters, offered to prove the mental capacity of the person to whom they were written, were inadmissible hearsay.

ISSUE: Are hearsay statements offered to establish a fact based upon the opinion of the declarant admissible?

HOLDING AND DECISION: (Parke, B.) No. Hearsay statements offered to establish a fact based upon the opinion of the declarant are inadmissible. The statements contained in the letters were made outside of court and were offered to prove the truth of the statements. The purpose behind the introduction of the statements into evidence was to show the declarant felt that the person to whom the letters were written, Marsden, had the legal capacity to understand and carry on his own affairs. These facts were relevant only as implying a statement or opinion of a third person on a matter in issue and are thus inadmissible where such statement or opinion would of itself be inadmissible. The declarants or writers of the letters could not have come into court to testify that they made the statements previously, due to the hearsay rule. As a result, the letters were inadmissible. Reversed.

EDITOR'S ANALYSIS: This case represents an excellent example of nonassertive conduct as hearsay. The statements in the letters themselves were not necessarily offered on face value to prove their truth. It was what was to be implied from the statements which did not offer the requisite level of reliability to allow them to overcome the hearsay prohibition. The court likened the written statements to spoken words which if offered for their truth would likewise be inadmissible hearsay.

QUICKNOTES

HEARSAY - An out-of-court statement made by a person other than the witness testifying at trial that is offered in order to prove the truth of the matter asserted.

NOTES:

CAIN v. GEORGE
Parents of deceased child (P) v. Hotel owner (D)
411 F.2d 572 (5th Cir. 1969).

NATURE OF CASE: Appeal of denial of damages for wrongful death.

FACT SUMMARY: A trial court admitted evidence of a lack of prior complaints about an allegedly defective heater.

CONCISE RULE OF LAW: Evidence regarding complaints is not hearsay.

FACTS: The Cains' (P) child was found dead in a hotel room. He was lying near a smoldering chair which was adjacent to a heater. The cause of death was carbon monoxide poisoning. The Cains (P) sued, contending that the source of the gas was the heater. George (D), the hotel owner, contended this was not so. The trial court permitted George (D) to testify, over the Cains' (P) hearsay objection, that there had been no prior complaints regarding the heater. The jury rendered a defense verdict, and the Cains (P) appealed.

ISSUE: Is evidence regarding complaints hearsay?

HOLDING AND DECISION: (Per curiam) No. Evidence regarding complaints is not hearsay. Such evidence is not dependent on the veracity and credibility of the would-be declarants, but rather on that of the testifying witness. This being so, the policy implications of hearsay do not arise and excluding such evidence is not proper. Affirmed.

EDITOR'S ANALYSIS: The rule might be different if evidence regarding complaints, as opposed to a lack of complaints, was at issue. In that case, out-of-court statements would be sought as an admission. Whether such statements would be classified hearsay is debatable; also, there is a good chance an exception, such as business records, could be found.

QUICKNOTES
HEARSAY - An out-of-court statement made by a person other than the witness testifying at trial that is offered in order to prove the truth of the matter asserted.

UNITED STATES v. CHECK
Government (P) v. Convicted drug-dealing police officer (D)
582 F.2d 668 (1978).

NATURE OF CASE: Appeal from conviction of possession of cocaine with intent to distribute.

FACT SUMMARY: In a prosecution based on possession of cocaine, the State (P) attempted to circumvent the hearsay rule by suggesting what an unavailable declarant said.

CONCISE RULE OF LAW: The hearsay rule cannot be circumvented by framing testimony so as to suggest what an unavailable declarant said.

FACTS: As part of an internal investigation of police officer Check (D), undercover officer Spinelli had dealings with one Cali, who made statements tending to incriminate Check (D). Check (D) was charged with possession of cocaine with intent to distribute. Cali was unavailable to testify. The State (P) elicited testimony from Spinelli, on direct, as to his conversations with Cali. While Spinelli did not quote Cali, he quoted his responses to Cali, responses that suggested what Cali had said. Check (D) was convicted and he appealed.

ISSUE: Can the hearsay rule be circumvented by framing testimony so as to suggest what an unavailable declarant said?

HOLDING AND DECISION: (Waterman, J.) No. The hearsay rule cannot be circumvented by framing testimony so as to suggest what an unavailable declarant said. When testimony is framed so as to lead to out-of-court statements being introduced to prove their own truth, the hearsay rule is invoked, even if the statements are not directly quoted. This was the case here. In substance, Cali's statements were introduced although they were not introduced verbatim. Reversed.

EDITOR'S ANALYSIS: The case stands for the proposition that hearsay can be a subtle thing. Often, words or acts will suggest something which is itself hearsay. Unless a reason to introduce the words or acts for something other than the hearsay purpose can be found, exclusion is proper.

QUICKNOTES
HEARSAY - An out-of-court statement made by a person other than the witness testifying at trial that is offered in order to prove the truth of the matter asserted.

UNITED STATES v. SINGER
Government (P) v. Convicted drug dealer (D)
687 F.2d 1135, modified en banc, 710 F.2d 431 (8th Cir. 1983).

NATURE OF CASE: Appeal of conviction for drug-related offenses.

FACT SUMMARY: Sazenski (D) raised a hearsay objection to the introduction of evidence of conduct not intended as an assertion.

CONCISE RULE OF LAW: Evidence of conduct not intended as an assertion of fact is not made inadmissible by the hearsay rule.

FACTS: Sazenski (D) and Izquierdo (D) roomed together. Izquierdo (D) used the alias "Carlos Almaden." They were prosecuted for various drug-related offenses. At one point, the Government (P) introduced a letter addressed to Sazenski (D) and "Carlos Almaden" to prove they shared a residence. Sazenski's (D) hearsay objection was overruled. Sazenski (D) was convicted, and he appealed.

ISSUE: Is evidence of conduct not intended as an assertion of fact made inadmissible by the hearsay rule?

HOLDING AND DECISION: (Henley, J.) No. Evidence of conduct not intended as an assertion of fact is not made inadmissible by the hearsay rule. When evidence of conduct tends to demonstrate behavior based on a belief, the untrustworthiness implications of the hearsay rule are not brought into play. People tend to conform their behavior to their beliefs. Here, the writer of the letter addressed it as he did because of a belief that Sazenski (D) and "Carlos Almaden" lived at that address together. Evidence of this was not hearsay. Affirmed.

EDITOR'S ANALYSIS: "Hearsay" is defined only to include "statements." Technically, behavior is not a statement. However, it has been established for a long time that conduct can be, if conditions are met, tantamount to verbal assertions for purposes of the hearsay.

QUICKNOTES
HEARSAY - An out-of-court statement made by a person other than the witness testifying at trial that is offered in order to prove the truth of the matter asserted.

NOTES:

UNITED STATES v. PACELLI
Government (P) v. Convicted murderer (D)
491 F.2d 1108 (2d Cir. 1974).

NATURE OF CASE: Appeal of a conviction for civil rights violation.

FACT SUMMARY: Pacelli (D) raised a hearsay objection to the introduction of statements implying facts asserted to prove their own truth.

CONCISE RULE OF LAW: Testimony regarding statements which imply facts presented to prove their own truth is hearsay.

FACTS: Pacelli (D) was charged with violating the civil rights of one Parks, whom he allegedly murdered. At trial, the Government (P) introduced certain statements of associates of Pacelli (D) which, although not directly saying that Pacelli (D) committed the murder, clearly implied this belief. Pacelli's (D) hearsay objection was overruled. He was convicted, and he appealed.

ISSUE: Is testimony regarding statements which imply facts presented to prove their own truth hearsay?

HOLDING AND DECISION: (Mansfield, J.) Yes. Testimony regarding statements which imply facts presented to prove their own truth is hearsay. When extra-judicial statements imply knowledge and belief on the part of nontestifying declarants as to material facts and are introduced to prove their own truth, the hearsay rule is directly implicated. Here, the statements made by the nontestifying declarants implied belief that Pacelli (D) committed the murder, and no purpose other than establishing this fact was served by the statements' introduction. This was clearly a hearsay violation. Reversed.

DISSENT: (Moore, J.) As no declarant actually expressed an opinion that Pacelli (D) committed the murder, the hearsay rule was not implicated.

EDITOR'S ANALYSIS: The opinion and dissent basically disagree as to how far the hearsay rule may go. The dissent would limit it to actual assertions. The majority was of the view that the rule could be invoked when the fact in question is merely implied.

NOTES:

QUICKNOTES
HEARSAY - An out-of-court statement made by a person other than the witness testifying at trial that is offered in order to prove the truth of the matter asserted.

BETTS v. BETTS
Father (P) v. Mother (D)
Wash. Ct. of App., 473 P.2d 403 (1970).

NATURE OF CASE: Appeal of child custody order.

FACT SUMMARY: In a custody hearing, the court admitted testimony regarding statements by the child which were relevant whether or not they were true.

CONCISE RULE OF LAW: Statements which are relevant whether or not they are true do not implicate the hearsay rule.

FACTS: Rita Betts (D), after divorcing Michael Betts (P), was awarded custody of their children. Rita (D) began living with Caporale. Not long after, one of the children died from severe injuries. Caporale was tried for murder and acquitted. The other child was placed in a foster home. Michael (P) commenced a custody proceeding. At the proceeding, the foster mother testified as to the child's statements that Caporale had killed her brother and would kill her as well. Rita's (D) hearsay objection was overruled. Michael (P) was awarded custody, and Rita (D) appealed.

ISSUE: Do statements which are relevant whether or not they are true implicate the hearsay rule?

HOLDING AND DECISION: (Armstrong, C.J.) No. Statements relevant whether or not they are true do not implicate the hearsay rule. The rule relates to out-of-court statements which are admitted to prove their own truth. When they are relevant, whether or not they are true, the rule necessarily is inapplicable. Here, the testimony regarding the child's statements was relevant to the issue of how being placed in the same house as Caporale would affect her. Whether her beliefs in this regard were true would be largely irrelevant as to this issue, and therefore the statements were not hearsay. Affirmed.

EDITOR'S ANALYSIS: Because the statements by the child were held not to be hearsay, the necessity of discussing exceptions thereto did not arise. Several exceptions probably could have been found had this been necessary. The most obvious would have been the "state-of-mind" exception. The "excited utterance" exception might also apply.

NOTES:

4

CHAPTER 4
HEARSAY EXCEPTIONS

QUICK REFERENCE RULES OF LAW

1. **Prior Inconsistent Statements.** A sworn statement inconsistent with courtroom testimony maybe substantively introduced if reliable. (State v. Smith)

2. **Prior Consistent Statements.** Fed. R. Evid. 801(d)(1)(B) permits prior consistent statements to be used for substantive purposes after the statements are admitted to rebut the existence of an improper influence or motive. (Tome v. United States)

3. **Prior Statements of Identification.** A composite sketch is not made inadmissible by the hearsay rule. (State v. Motta)

4. **Individual Admissions.** The conviction of a defendant at a joint trial must be set aside despite a jury instruction that a co-defendant's confession incriminating the defendant must be disregarded in determining his guilt or innocence. (Bruton v. United States)

5. **Adoptive Admissions.** Where one of the parties to the action has manifested his adoption of or belief in the truth of a statement that would otherwise constitute hearsay, it is admissible under an exception to the hearsay rule for admissions by a party opponent. (United States v. Hoosier)

6. **Adoptive Admissions.** A state may not impeach a defendant's exculpatory story by noting his failure to tell the same story upon arrest. (Doyle v. Ohio)

7. **Admissions by Employees and Agents.** Fed. R. Evid. 801(d)(2)(D) makes statements made by agents within the scope of their employment admissible and there is no implied requirement that the declarant have personal knowledge of the facts underlying his statement. (Mahlandt v. Wild Candid Survival & Research Center)

8. **Coconspirator Statements.** A court may, in determining whether a conspiracy existed, consider the out-of-court statements which themselves are the subject of the inquiry into admissibility. (Bourjaily v. United States)

9. **Present Sense Impressions and Excited Utterances.** In an action based on forcing an ill employee to work, testimony regarding the employee's conversations with the employer may be admissible. (Nuttall v. Reading Co.)

10. **Present Sense Impressions.** A lapse of time or the fact the out-of-court statement was made in response to an inquiry, does not necessarily remove the excited utterance hearsay exception of Fed. R. Evid. 803(2). (United States v. Iron Shell)

11. **Subsequent Conduct.** Whenever an intention is of itself a distinct and material fact in a chain of circumstances, it may be proved by contemporaneous oral or written declarations of the party. (Mutual Life Insurance Co. v. Hillmon)

12. **Subsequent Conduct.** Hearsay evidence of statements in which the declarant has stated his intention to do something with another person are admissible under the state of mind exception to the hearsay rule to show that he intended to do it, from which the trier of fact may draw the inference that he carried out his intention and did it. (United States v. Pheaster)

13. **Statements to Physicians.** A statement by a child victim to a medical professional is admissible in situations involving physical or sexual abuse of the child. (Blake v. State)

14. **Past Recollection Recorded.** The prior recorded statement of a witness in a criminal trial can be admitted under the exception to the hearsay rule for records of "past recollection recorded," and such does not violate the defendant's Sixth Amendment right of confrontation. (Ohio v. Scott)

15. **Business Records.** For a portion of a business record to be admissible, the source of the information contained therein must be known. (Petrocelli v. Gallison)

16. **Business Records.** Information that is otherwise hearsay may be admissible under the ordinary business records exception, so long as all of the persons furnishing the information to be recorded are acting in the regular course of business. (Norcon, Inc. v. Kotowski)

17. **Public Records.** When they result from an investigation made pursuant to authority granted by law, factual findings (including evaluations and opinions) in public records and reports are admissible unless the sources of information or other circumstances indicate lack of trustworthiness. (Baker v. Elcona Homes Corp.)

18. **Public Records.** In criminal cases, reports of public agencies setting forth factual findings resulting from investigations made pursuant to authority granted by law are inadmissible hearsay and not subject to any exception if the reports are sought to be introduced against the accused. (United States v. Oates)

19. **The Unavailability Requirement.** A witness is not unavailable for purposes of the prior testimony exception to the confrontation requirement unless the prosecutorial authorities have made a good faith effort to obtain his presence at trial. (Barber v. Page)

20. **The Former Testimony Exception.** The prior testimony of an unavailable witness is admissible under Fed. R. Evid. 804(b)(1) if the party against whom it is offered or a "predecessor in interest" had the "opportunity and similar motive to develop the testimony by direct, cross or redirect examination." (Lloyd v. American Export Lines, Inc.)

21. **Criminal Cases—Statements Implicating the Accused.** Fed. R. Evid. 804(b)(3) does not allow admission of non-self-inculpatory statements, even if they are made within a broader narrative that is generally self-inculpatory. (Williamson v. United States)

22. **The Catchall and Proof of Exonerating Facts.** In making a trustworthiness determination, the court must consider the declarant's propensity to tell the truth, whether the alleged statements were made under oath, assurances of the declarant's personal knowledge, the time lapse between the event and the statement concerning the event, and the motivations of the declarant. (State v. Weaver)

23. **Constitution as Bar Against Hearsay.** The right to confrontation is not violated by the presentation of the transcript testimony where there was an adequate opportunity to cross-examine the witness at the official proceeding where the testimony was given. (Ohio v. Roberts)

24. **Constitution as Bar Against Hearsay.** Where testimonial statements are at issue, the only indicium of reliability sufficient to satisfy constitutional demands is the one the Constitution actually prescribes: confrontation. (Crawford v. Washington)

25. **"New Hearsay."** Extrinsic evidence of the reliability of hearsay statements of an alleged child abuse victim may not be considered by a court in deciding upon the admissibility of the statement. (Idaho v. Wright)

STATE v. SMITH

State (P) v. Convicted assailant (D)

Wash. Sup. Ct., 651 P.2d 207 (1982).

NATURE OF CASE: Appeal of order granting new trial following conviction for assault.

FACT SUMMARY: A sworn statement by assault victim Conlin was admitted as an inconsistent statement after she refused, at trial, to identify Smith (D) as her attacker, as she had earlier done.

CONCISE RULE OF LAW: A sworn statement inconsistent with courtroom testimony may be substantively introduced if reliable.

FACTS: Conlin was assaulted and severely battered in a motel room. At first she identified Smith (D), with whom she lived, as the assailant. She wrote out a statement identifying him as the perpetrator, and then signed it under penalty of perjury. At trial, however, she changed her testimony and stated that another man was responsible. The trial court permitted the prosecution to introduce the statement substantively, over Smith's (D) hearsay objection. Smith (D) was convicted. The court, changing its mind regarding the admissibility of the statement, ordered a new trial. The prosecution appealed.

ISSUE: May a sworn statement inconsistent with courtroom testimony be substantively introduced if reliable?

HOLDING AND DECISION: (Dimmick, J.) Yes. A sworn statement inconsistent with courtroom testimony may be substantively introduced if reliable. Fed. R. Evid. 801(d)(1)(a), adopted in the State of Washington, permits the substantive introduction of prior inconsistent statements if given under oath at a trial, hearing, deposition, or "other proceeding." What constitutes an "other proceeding" is not defined. The usual approach, which this court adopts, is to analyze each situation on an ad hoc basis to decide on admissibility. Reliability is the key. Here, the inconsistent statement was made while the incident was fresh in Conlin's mind, before she had a chance to forget or be intimidated into changing her story. This demonstrates reliability on the part of the statement, and its admission was proper. Reversed.

EDITOR'S ANALYSIS: The present form of Fed. R. Evid. 801(d)(1)(a) came about as a compromise. The Senate version would have permitted the substantive admission of all inconsistent statements. The House versions would have permitted only those made in grand jury proceedings.

QUICKNOTES

HEARSAY - An out-of-court statement made by a person other than the witness testifying at trial that is offered in order to prove the truth of the matter asserted.

NOTES:

TOME v. UNITED STATES

Convicted sexual abuser (D) v. Government (P)

513 U.S. 150 (1995).

NATURE OF CASE: Appeal from conviction of felony sexual abuse of a child.

FACT SUMMARY: Tome (D), convicted of felony sexual abuse of a child, appealed, contending that the trial court abused its discretion by admitting out-of-court consistent statements made by his daughter to six prosecution witnesses who testified as to the nature of Tome's (D) sexual assaults on his daughter.

CONCISE RULE OF LAW: Fed. R. Evid. 801(d)(1)(B) permits prior consistent statements to be used for substantive purposes after the statements are admitted to rebut the existence of an improper influence or motive.

FACTS: Tome (D) was charged by the United States (P) with felony sexual abuse of his daughter, A.T., who was four years old at the time of the alleged crime. Tome (D) and the child's mother were divorced in 1988, and the mother was finally awarded custody in 1990. Thereafter, the mother contacted authorities with allegations that Tome (D) had committed sexual abuse against A.T. Tome (D) argued that A.T.'s allegations were concocted so that the child would not be returned to Tome (D) for visitation purposes. At trial, A.T. testified first for the United States (P). Thereafter, cross-examination took place over two trial days. On the first day, A.T. answered all questions placed to her. Under cross-examination, however, A.T. was questioned regarding her conversations with the prosecutor but was reluctant to discuss them. The United States (P) then produced six witnesses who testified about seven statements made by A.T. describing Tome's (D) sexual assaults upon her. A.T.'s out-of-court statements, recounted by these witnesses, were offered by the United States (P) under Fed. R. Evid. 801(d)(1)(B). The trial court admitted all of the statements over Tome's (D) objections, accepting the United State's (P) argument that they rebutted the implicit charges that A.T.'s testimony was motivated by a desire to live with her mother. Tome (D) was convicted and sentenced to twelve years' imprisonment. On appeal, the Tenth Circuit Court of Appeals affirmed, and Tome (D) again appealed, contending that the district court judge had abused his discretion in admitting A.T.'s out-of-court statements.

ISSUE: Does Fed. R. Evid. 801(d)(1)(B) permit prior consistent statements to be used for substantive purposes after the statements are admitted to rebut the existence of an improper motive?

HOLDING AND DECISION: (Kennedy, J.) Yes. Fed. R. Evid. 801(d)(1)(B) permits prior consistent statements to be used for substantive purposes after the statements are admitted to rebut the existence of an improper motive. The prevailing common law rule, before adoption of the Federal Rules of Evidence, was that a prior consistent statement introduced to rebut a charge of recent fabrication or improper influence or motive was admissible if the statement had been made before the alleged fabrication, influence, or motive came into being but inadmissible if made afterward. Rule 801 defines prior consistent statements as nonhearsay only if they are offered to rebut a charge of recent fabrication or improper influence or motive. Prior consistent statements may not be admitted to counter all forms of impeachment or to bolster the witness merely because she has been discredited. Here, the question is whether A.T.'s out-of-court statements rebutted the alleged link between her desire to be with her mother and her testimony, not whether they suggested that A.T.'s testimony was true. The Rule speaks of a party's rebutting an alleged motive, not bolstering the veracity of the story told. However, the requirement is that consistent statements must have been made before the alleged influence or motive to fabricate arose. The language of the Rule suggests that it was intended to carry over the common law premotive rule. If the Rule were to permit introduction of prior statements as substantive evidence to rebut every implicit charge that a witness' in-court testimony results from recent fabrication, improper influence, or motive, the whole emphasis of the trial could shift to the out-of-court statements rather than the in-court ones. In response to a rather weak charge that A.T.'s testimony was a fabrication so that she could stay with her mother, the United States (P) was allowed to present a parade of witnesses who did no more than recount A.T.'s detailed out-of-court statements to them. Although those statements might have been probative on the question of whether the alleged conduct had occurred, they shed minimal light on whether A.T. had the charged motive to fabricate. Reversed and remanded.

CONCURRENCE: (Scalia, J.) The approach taken by the Advisory Committee Notes to interpret the Fed. R. Evid. is wrong and contains "no special authoritativeness as the work of the draftsmen." The text of Fed. R. Evid. 801(d)(1)(B) is of greatest significance because it follows the common law approach and would produce a contradictory result if any other approach were followed instead.

DISSENT: (Breyer, J.) The majority incorrectly base their decision on the premise that the basic issue in the case is hearsay, rather than relevance. Relying on timing as a factor when deciding the reliability of a statement is incorrect. The

Continued on next page.

language of Fed. R. Evid. (801)(d)(1)(B) should be taken at face value. Fed. R. Evid. 801(d)(1)(B) does not support the majority assertion that the statements used to rehabilitate must have been made before the charge of recent fabrication or improper influence or motive. Whether a statement was made before or after a witness has been cross-examined relates to the probative value of the statement, but not to its reliability. In addition, the Fed. R. Evid. differed from the common law in many respects to allow more case by case discretion, so this rationale is not a valid one either.

EDITOR'S ANALYSIS: Justice Breyer, in his dissent, commented that prior consistent statements may rehabilitate a witness whose credibility has been questioned. Justice Breyer also cited Judge Friendly's opinion in *United States v. Rubin*, 609 F.2d 51 (2d Cir. 1979). In that case, Judge Friendly argued that Rule 801(d)(1)(B)'s timing requirement applied exclusively to those prior consistent statements offered for their truth after a challenge of recent fabrication or improper influence or motive. When used just to rehabilitate after other varieties of challenge and credibility, the statement is admissible under Rule 801(c) for a limited purpose of questioning credibility rather than for the truth of the statement. Friendly argued that Rule 801(d)(1)(B)'s timing restrictions were inapplicable. In these circumstances, no improper influence or motive is alleged, and the prior statement does not need to precede it.

QUICKNOTES

CONSENT - A voluntary and willful agreement by an individual possessing sufficient mental capacity to undertake an action suggested by another.

NOTES:

STATE v. MOTTA
State (P) v. Convicted robber (D)
Haw. Sup. Ct., 659 P.2d 745 (1983).

NATURE OF CASE: Appeal of conviction for robbery.

FACT SUMMARY: Motta (D) was convicted of robbery after a composite sketch was admitted into evidence.

CONCISE RULE OF LAW: A composite sketch is not made inadmissible by the hearsay rule.

FACTS: Iwashita was robbed at gunpoint. Soon thereafter, based on her description of the perpetrator, a composite sketch was made by a police artist. Iwashita later picked out Motta's (D) photo from a series of mug shots. At trial, Iwashita identified Motta (D) as the assailant. The sketch was admitted as substantive evidence over Motta's (D) hearsay objection. Motta (D) was convicted, and he appealed.

ISSUE: Is a composite sketch made inadmissible by the hearsay rule?

HOLDING AND DECISION: (Lum, C.J.) No. A composite sketch is not made inadmissible by the hearsay rule. Some courts have declined to consider such evidence as hearsay. This court is not so inclined because such a sketch is properly considered the product of out-of-court statements whose only relevance is their own truth. However, Fed. R. Evid. 801(d)(1)(c), adopted in this state, permits the substantive introduction of prior identifications as a hearsay exception, as long as the identifying individual is available for cross-examination. As the sketch was a result of identification and both Iwashita and the artist were available, the requirements of the rule were met. Affirmed.

EDITOR'S ANALYSIS: Motta (D) argued that the sketch was in essence a corroboration of Iwashita's testimony. Such evidence, argued Motta (D), should be admitted only to rebut impeaching evidence, of which none existed. The court rejected this, holding that the sketch was substantively admissible and not merely a vehicle for rehabilitation.

QUICKNOTES
HEARSAY RULE - Rule that an out-of-court statement made by a person, other than the witness testifying at trial and that is offered in order to prove the truth of the matter asserted, is inadmissible.

NOTES:

BRUTON v. UNITED STATES
Convicted robber (D) v. Government (P)
391 U.S. 123 (1968).

NATURE OF CASE: Appeal from conviction for robbery.

FACT SUMMARY: The Government (P) contended that Bruton's (D) robbery conviction based upon the confession of a co-conspirator was valid.

CONCISE RULE OF LAW: The conviction of a defendant at a joint trial must be set aside despite a jury instruction that a co-defendant's confession incriminating the defendant must be disregarded in determining his guilt or innocence.

FACTS: Evans was arrested and charged with armed postal robbery. In the course of his confinement, he orally confessed to the postal authorities that both he and Bruton (D) committed the robbery. A joint trial was held wherein Evans' confession was admitted into evidence. The court instructed the jury that while the confession was substantive evidence against Evans, it could not be used to determine the guilt of Bruton (D). Both individuals were convicted, and Evans' conviction was overturned when it was determined that his confession should not be used against him. However, Bruton's (D) conviction was affirmed based upon the trial judge's limiting instruction. Bruton (D) appealed, contending the use of the confession in a joint trial constituted reversible error as to his conviction.

ISSUE: Must the conviction of a defendant at a joint trial be set aside despite a trial court's limiting instruction that the confession of a co-defendant cannot be used as substantive evidence?

HOLDING AND DECISION: (Brennan, J.) Yes. The conviction of a defendant at a joint trial must be set aside despite a jury instruction that a co-defendant's confession incriminating the defendant must be disregarded in determining his guilt or innocence. The use of such a confession presents a substantial risk that the jury, despite the instructions to the contrary, will look to the incriminating extra-judicial statements in determining a defendant's guilt. As a result, the use in the case of the confession deprived Bruton (D) of his right of cross-examination under the confrontation clause of the Sixth Amendment. Although there are many circumstances wherein the reliance upon the jury's following the court's order to disregard certain pieces of evidence and to use it only for particular purposes will be harmless, some pieces of evidence are so prejudicial as to require their exclusion. The risk of misuse is simply too high where such use potentially robs the co-defendant of his constitutional rights. Further, the confession of a co-defendant is so lacking in reliability with regard to the nonconfessing defendant that the hearsay rule must be strictly applied. Reversed.

DISSENT: (White, J.) The practical result of the Court's opinion in this case is to severely limit the ability of prosecutors to hold joint trials for defendants. The great value in using an uncoerced admission against one defendant when that would render the codefendant's conviction questionable will surely dissuade prosecutors from joint trials. This will greatly increase the judicial workload and the benefits of joint trials will be lost.

EDITOR'S ANALYSIS: There is no question that the use of a co-defendant's admission against another defendant is clearly hearsay. It is an out-of-court statement offered for its truth. It also contains several elements of unreliability including the fact that it is made under a stressful condition and usually made in an attempt to exalt the declarant at the expense of the co-defendant. As a result of this unreliability, the court is unwilling to allow it into evidence at all in a joint trial. Even though, as the dissent points out, there are great benefits to using an uncoerced confession against the declarant, many commentators have indicated that this benefit is clearly outweighed by the risk of the nondeclarant defendant's loss of his constitutional rights.

QUICKNOTES

REVERSIBLE ERROR - A substantial error that might reasonably have prejudiced the party complaining.

SIXTH AMENDMENT - Provides the right to a speedy trial by impartial jury, the right to be informed of the accusation, to confront witnesses and to have the assistance of counsel in all criminal prosecutions.

NOTES:

UNITED STATES v. HOOSIER
Government (P) v. Convicted robber (D)
542 F.2d 687 (6th Cir. 1976).

NATURE OF CASE: Appeal from a conviction for armed robbery.

FACT SUMMARY: A witness at Hoosier's (D) trial for armed robbery was permitted to testify to certain statements Hoosier's (D) girlfriend had made in Hoosier's (D) presence and to which he had offered no denial.

CONCISE RULE OF LAW: Where one of the parties to the action has manifested his adoption of or belief in the truth of a statement that would otherwise constitute hearsay, it is admissible under an exception to the hearsay rule for admissions by a party opponent.

FACTS: Hoosier (D) was convicted of armed robbery in a trial where the court allowed a witness to testify as to certain statements by Hoosier's (D) girlfriend. Hoosier (D) argued they constituted inadmissible hearsay. The witness testified that he saw Hoosier (D) and his girlfriend three weeks after the robbery and that Hoosier (D) had money and was wearing diamond rings. He further testified that the girlfriend had commented on Hoosier's (D) affluence, telling the witness, "That ain't nothing, you should have seen the money we had in the hotel room," thereafter speaking of "sacks of money." In the face of these statements, Hoosier (D) made no denial or other comment.

ISSUE: Can a statement which would otherwise be hearsay be admitted against a party to the action who manifested his adoption of or belief in the truth of the statement?

HOLDING AND DECISION: (Per curiam) Yes. There is an exception to the hearsay rule for admission by a party opponent, and it allows introduction into evidence of a statement which would otherwise constitute hearsay where one of the parties to the action had manifested his adoption of or belief in the truth of that statement. Adoption or acquiescence in the statement of another can be manifested in any appropriate manner—including failure to protest an untrue statement made in one's presence when such a protest would normally be forthcoming under the circumstances were the statement untrue. In such case, the decision calls for an evaluation in terms of probable human behavior. In this case, there is little likelihood that Hoosier's (D) silence in the face of his girlfriend's statements was due to "advice of counsel" or assertion of his Fifth Amendment right to remain silent. Under the total circumstances, probable human behavior would have been for him to deny her statements were they not true. Thus, admission of the statements was proper. Affirmed.

EDITOR'S ANALYSIS: Use of much of this type of evidence in criminal cases has been circumscribed by the constitutional restraints of Miranda and its progeny. When accusations are made, a defendant's failure to respond will usually be the result of his having been informed that his utterances might be used against him and it is his right to remain silent. Thus, use of this type of silence to admit such accusations would be unconstitutional.

QUICKNOTES

FIFTH AMENDMENT - Provides that no person shall be compelled to serve as a witness against himself, or be subject to trial for the same offense twice, or be deprived of life, liberty, or property without due process of law.

HEARSAY RULE - Rule that an out-of-court statement made by a person, other than the witness testifying at trial and that is offered in order to prove the truth of the matter asserted, is inadmissible.

NOTES:

DOYLE v. OHIO
Convicted drug dealer (D) v. Government (P)
426 U.S. 610 (1976).

NATURE OF CASE: Review of conviction for selling narcotics.

FACT SUMMARY: The prosecution attempted to impeach drug offense defendant Doyle's (D) exculpatory story by noting his failure to tell the same story upon arrest.

CONCISE RULE OF LAW: A state may not impeach a defendant's exculpatory story by noting his failure to tell the same story upon arrest.

FACTS: Through the use of a "plant," police were able to observe a purported sale of marijuana by Doyle (D), who was subsequently arrested. At trial, Doyle (D) offered an exculpatory version of events. The prosecution, upon cross-examination, inquired as to why he had not told the same story upon arrest. He had been given Miranda warnings. Doyle (D) was convicted, and the conviction was upheld on state appeal. The Supreme Court granted review.

ISSUE: May a state impeach a defendant's exculpatory story by noting his failure to tell the same story upon arrest?

HOLDING AND DECISION: (Powell, J.) No. A state may not impeach a defendant's exculpatory story by noting his failure to tell the same story upon arrest. When an arrestee, given his Miranda warnings, chooses to remain silent, no inference of guilt may arise from this. To hold otherwise would make these rights meaningless. While the warning contains no express assurance that silence carries no penalty, an arrestee may properly infer this. Therefore, to permit a defendant to be cross-examined regarding post-arrest silence, as Doyle (D) was here, violates due process. Reversed.

DISSENT: (Stevens, J.) Silence in matters such as this is tantamount to a prior inconsistent statement and should be admissible as impeachment.

EDITOR'S ANALYSIS: The key to this decision was the actual informing of the suspect that he had the right to be silent. This was tantamount to a promise that silence would place no peril upon the arrestee. The Court later, in *Jenkins v. Anderson*, 447 U.S. 231 (1980), declined to extend the rule to cover prearrest silence. Prearrest matters do not implicate the Miranda warning.

QUICKNOTES
IMPEACHMENT - The discrediting of a witness by offering evidence to show that the witness lacks credibility.

NOTES:

MAHLANDT v. WILD CANID SURVIVAL & RESEARCH CENTER

Injured child (P) v. Animal center (D)
588 F.2d 626 (8th Cir. 1978).

NATURE OF CASE: Appeal from denial of damages for negligence.

FACT SUMMARY: The trial court hearing Daniel Mahlandt's (P) civil action against the Center (D) refused to let into evidence certain conclusionary statements against interest made by an employee of the Center (D).

CONCISE RULE OF LAW: Fed. R. Evid. 801(d)(2)(D) makes statements made by agents within the scope of their employment admissible and there is no implied requirement that the declarant have personal knowledge of the facts underlying his statement.

FACTS: Nobody actually saw what happened, but young Daniel Mahlandt (P), who was just under four years old at the time, wound up in the enclosure where Kenneth Poos (D), the Director of the Center (D), kept Sophie, a wolf belonging to the Center (D) tame enough to take to schools and institutions where he showed films and gave programs on the nature of wolves. Sophie had been raised at the children's zoo and demonstrated a good nature and stable manner while in contact with thousands of children. Sophie apparently bit Mahlandt (P) causing him serious injuries. There was some evidence indicating that the child might havereceived his injuries crawling under the fence. An effort to disprove this theory was made by introducing evidence that Poos (D) had left a note on the door of the Center's (D) president saying a wolf had bitten a child and that he had made a similar statement later that day when he met the president and was asked what happened. There was also an offer to introduce minutes of a meeting of the Center's (D) board that reflected a great deal of discussion about the legal aspects of the incident of Sophie biting the child. None of this was admitted into evidence, the judge reasoning that in each case those making the statements had no personal knowledge of the facts and the statements were thus hearsay. A judgment for the Center (D) followed.

ISSUE: Is it necessary to show that the agent had personal knowledge of the facts underlining his statement for a statement made by an agent within the scope of his employment to be admissible under Fed. R. Evid. 801(d)(2)(D)?

HOLDING AND DECISION: (Van Sickle, J.) No. Fed. R. Evid. 801(d)(2)(D) makes admissible statements made by agents within the scope of their employment. Rule 403 provides for the exclusion of relevant evidence if its probative value is substantially outweighed by the danger of unfair prejudice, etc.

Rule 805 recites, in effect, that a statement containing hearsay within hearsay is admissible if each part of the statement falls within an exception to the hearsay rule. While each provided additional bases for excluding otherwise acceptable evidence, neither rule mandates the introduction into Rule 801 (d)(2)(D) of an implied requirement that the declarant have personal knowledge of the facts underlying his statement. Thus, the two statements made by Poos (D) (one in the note he wrote and one he made verbally) were admissible against the Center (D). As to the minutes of the Center's (D) board meeting, there was no servant or agency relationship which justified admitting the evidence of these minutes as against Poos (D) (who was a non-attending, non-participating employee). The only remaining question is whether the trial court's rulings excluding these three items of evidence are at all justified under Rule 403. It is true that none of the statements involved were based on the personal knowledge of the declarant. However, it was recognized by the Advisory Committee on Proposed Rules that this does not necessarily mean they must be rejected as too unreliable to be admitted into evidence. In its discussion of 801(d)(2) exceptions to the hearsay rule, the Committee said: "The freedom which admissions have enjoyed from technical demands of searching for an assurance of trustworthiness in some against-interest circumstances, and from the restrictive influences of the opinion rule and the rule requiring first-hand knowledge, when taken with the apparently prevalent satisfaction with the results, calls for generous treatment of this avenue to admissibility." 28 U.S.C.A., Volume of Federal Rules of Evidence, Rule 801, p. 527, at p. 530. So here, remembering that relevant evidence is usually prejudicial to the cause of the side against which it is presented, and that the prejudice which concerns us is unreasonable prejudice—and applying the spirit of Rule 801 (d)(2)—Rule 403 does not warrant the exclusion of the evidence of Poos' (D) statements as against himself or the Center (D). But the limited admissibility of the corporate minutes, coupled with the repetitive nature of the evidence and the low probative value of the minute record, all justify supporting the judgment of the trial court, under Rule 403, not to admit them into evidence. Reversed and remanded for a new trial.

EDITOR'S ANALYSIS: One of the questions courts have struggled with in this area is whether or not in order to qualify as an admission the statement must have been made by the agent to an outsider (i.e., one other than his principal or another agent). This often comes up when the opposing party in a suit against the principal wants to introduce into evidence a report written or given orally by an agent to the principal or another agent. Just as many courts have refused to let such evidence in as have let it in against the principal as an admission. The Federal Rules of Evidence have been interpreted as recognizing what Wigmore observed: that "communication to an outsider has not generally been thought to be an essential characteristic of an admission." Wigmore on Evidence, § 1557.

BOURJAILY v. UNITED STATES
Conspirator (D) v. Government (P)
483 U.S. 171 (1987).

NATURE OF CASE: Appeal from conviction for conspiracy to distribute drugs.

FACT SUMMARY: Bourjaily (D) contended that the trial court erred in considering statements by an accomplice in determining whether a conspiracy existed, as such a finding was a prerequisite to determining the admissibility of the statements.

CONCISE RULE OF LAW: A court may, in determining whether a conspiracy existed, consider the out-of-court statements which themselves are the subject of the inquiry into admissibility.

FACTS: Bourjaily (D) was charged with conspiracy to distribute cocaine. The Government (P) introduced out-of-court statements made by Lonardo, an accomplice, which arguably implicated Bourjaily (D) in the conspiracy. Under Fed. R. Evid. 801, out-of-court statements by a co-conspirator against a party, made during the course of the conspiracy, are not hearsay. The court made a preliminary evidentiary ruling based in part on Lonardo's out-of-court statements, that a conspiracy existed and that Bourjaily (D) was a co-conspirator. This ruling was made solely as a preliminary step to determining whether the out-of-court statements fell under Rule 801, and were thus admissible. Bourjaily (D) was convicted and appealed, contending the court could not consider the statements themselves in determining whether a conspiracy existed where such determination was the threshold consideration in the statement's admissibility.

ISSUE: May a court, in making a preliminary determination of admissibility under Fed. R. Evid. 801, consider the subject statements?

HOLDING AND DECISION: (Rehnquist, C.J.) Yes. A court may, in making a preliminary determination of admissibility under Fed. R. Evid. 801, consider the subject statements to determine if a conspiracy exists. Although case authority exists to the contrary, the amendments to the Federal Rules have made it clear that the statements may be used. Once it is shown by a preponderance of the evidence that a conspiracy existed and that the defendant was involved, the statements are not hearsay. The statements themselves may be highly probative of the existence of a conspiracy and may be used. Affirmed.

DISSENT: (Blackmun, J.) Evidence of a statement by an agent concerning the existence or extent of his authority is not admissible against the principal to prove its existence or extent unless it appears *by other evidence* that the making of such statement was within the authority of the agent or, as to persons dealing with the agent, within the apparent authority or other power of the agent. There was a common law recognition that this exemption from the hearsay rule had certain guarantees of trustworthiness, albeit limited ones. The Federal Rules of Evidence did not alter in any way this common law exemption to hearsay. Modernly, co-conspirator statements in some cases are, at best, nothing more than "idle chatter" of a declarant or, at worst, "malicious gossip." The independent evidence requirement is a necessary safeguard.

EDITOR'S ANALYSIS: Rule 104 allows trial courts to consider hearsay evidence in making evidentiary determinations. Thus, the Court read Rule 104 in conjunction with Rule 801 to arrive at its decision. It has been held, however, that if an agency relationship must be proved, the statements at issue cannot be considered.

QUICKNOTES

CONSPIRACY - Concerted action by two or more persons to accomplish some unlawful purpose.

FED. R. EVID. 104 - Permits a court to consider all nonprivileged matters, whether independently admissible or not, when determining preliminary issues of admissibility.

NOTES:

NUTTALL v. READING CO.
Wife of deceased (P) v. Employer (D)
235 F.2d 546 (3rd Cir. 1956).

NATURE OF CASE: Appeal of directed verdict dismissing action for damages under the Federal Employers' Liability Act.

FACT SUMMARY: Nuttall (P) attempted to introduce statements made by her late husband during a telephone conversation with his employer.

CONCISE RULE OF LAW: In an action based on forcing an ill employee to work, testimony regarding the employee's conversations with the employer may be admissible.

FACTS: Nuttall (P), executrix of her husband's estate, filed an action under the Federal Employers' Liability Act, (FELA), against his former employer, Reading Co. (D). At trial, Nuttall (P) sought to introduce testimony regarding a telephone conversation her husband had had with his supervisor on a particular day, when he had tried to phone in sick. His portion of the conversation suggested that the supervisor (who was also deceased) had forced him to come to work. The court refused the testimony and delivered a directed verdict in favor of Reading (D). Nuttall (P) appealed.

ISSUE: In an action based on forcing an ill employee to work, may testimony regarding the employee's conversations with the employer be admissible?

HOLDING AND DECISION: (Goodrich, J.) Yes. In an action based on forcing an ill employee to work, testimony regarding the employee's conversations with the employer may be admissible. An employer covered by the FELA may be liable for forcing an ill employee to work. Liability requires proof that the employee was coerced. Testimony regarding a conversation between the employee and the employer is probative on this issue and should be admitted. Reversed.

EDITOR'S ANALYSIS: The court here spoke in terms of hearsay, but did not identify which exception it was invoking to get by the hearsay problem. At least two are possible. These are present sense impressions, and the mental state exceptions. Which one the court applied here was unclear.

QUICKNOTES

RELEVANT EVIDENCE - Evidence having any tendency to prove or disprove a disputed fact.

UNITED STATES v. IRON SHELL
Government (P) v. Convicted assailant (D)
633 F.2d 77 (8th Cir. 1980)

NATURE OF CASE: Appeal from conviction for assault with intent to commit rape.

FACT SUMMARY: Iron Shell (D) argued that the trial judge abused his discretion in permitting a police officer to testify to the victim's statements as a hearsay exception under Fed. R. Evid. 803(2) when there was a delay between the statements and the event and the statements were made in response to an inquiry.

CONCISE RULE OF LAW: A lapse of time or the fact that the out-of-court statement was made in response to an inquiry, does not necessarily remove the excited utterance hearsay exception of Fed. R. Evid. 803(2).

FACTS: Lucy, a young girl, was found "crying and hollering" in the bushes. Mae Small Bear walked to the bushes and saw Lucy lying on her back with Iron Shell (D) lying beside her on his side. Lucy's jeans were down to her ankles, and she was "crying hard" and looked scared. Iron Shell (D) was observed trying to hide her. Lucy's face was swollen on one side. Lucy was taken to the police station about an hour later and interviewed by a police officer who asked her a single question: "What happened?" In response, Lucy said that Iron Shell (D) grabbed her and held her around the neck, telling her to be quiet or he would choke her. Lucy said Iron Shell (D) tried to remove her pants and "he tried to what you call it me." The officer testified to the above at trial, noting that Lucy had spoken to her in short bursts and appeared nervous and scared. A jury convicted Iron Shell (D) of assault with intent to commit rape. He appealed, arguing that the lapse of time and the fact that Lucy's out-of-court statements were made in response to an inquiry removed the excited utterance hearsay exception of Fed. R. Evid. 803(2) under which the police officer had been permitted to testify about Lucy's declarations to her.

ISSUE: Does a lapse of time, or the fact that the out-of-court statement was made in response to an inquiry, necessarily remove the excited utterance hearsay exception of Fed. R. Evid. 803(2)?

HOLDING AND DECISION: (Stephenson, J.) No. A lapse of time, or the fact the out-of-court statement was made in response to an inquiry, does not necessarily remove the excited utterance hearsay exception of Fed. R. Evid. 803(2). Here, the lapse of time between the starting event and the out-of-court statement, although relevant, is not dispositive in the application of Rule 803(2). Nor is it controlling that Lucy's statement was made in response to an inquiry. Rather, these are factors the trial court must weigh in determining whether the offered testimony is within the 803(2) exception. Other factors to consider include the age of the declarant, the physical and mental condition of the declarant, the characteristics of the event, and the subject matter of the statements. In order to find that 803(2) applies, it must appear that the declarant's condition at the time was such that the statement was spontaneous, excited, or impulsive, rather than the product of reflection and deliberation. Here, such determination is a close question. While there is testimony that Lucy was calm and unexcited, in contrast the same witness described her as "nervous and scared." Testimony suggested that Lucy had struggled with Iron Shell (D), that he had threatened her with serious harm, and that he had unsnapped and pulled down her jeans. The stress and fear that such an occurrence would impose upon a young girl cannot be discounted. Furthermore, Lucy did not give the police officer a detailed narrative but spoke in short bursts about the incident. Under the circumstances of the instant case, considering the surprise of the assault, its shocking nature, and the age of the declarant, it was not an abuse of discretion for the trial judge to permit the 803(2) hearsay exception. Affirmed.

EDITOR'S ANALYSIS: Fed. R. Evid. 803(2) allows the admission of hearsay, otherwise competent, that is a "statement relating to a startling event or condition made while the declarant was under the stress of excitement caused by the event or condition." Statements made in response to a police inquiry are sometimes considered not spontaneous because the product of reasoned reflection between the declarant and the questioner. The government, on the other hand, may argue that the statements are spontaneous because the declarant is still scared and nervous from the event.

QUICKNOTES

FED. R. EVID. 803 - Federal Rule of Evidence setting forth certain exceptions to the hearsay rule, including present sense impressions, excited utterances, present state of mind, statements for medical diagnosis, past recollection recorded, etc.

MUTUAL LIFE INSURANCE CO. v. HILLMON
Insurance company (D) v. Wife of decedent (P)
145 U.S. 285 (1892).

NATURE OF CASE: Appeal from judgment enforcing life insurance policies.

FACT SUMMARY: Mutual (D) contended that letters written by the person it claimed was the actual decedent and indicating that person's intention to accompany Hillmon, the purported decedent and insured, were relevant and admissible to prove a conspiracy theory that Hillmon had not died and therefore his wife was not entitled to the insurance proceeds.

CONCISE RULE OF LAW: Whenever an intention is of itself a distinct and material fact in a chain of circumstances, it may be proved by contemporaneous oral or written declarations of the party.

FACTS: Hillmon (P) sued to collect the proceeds of three separate life insurance policies. She contended that her husband, a cowboy and adventurer, had died in March 1879, when he was accidentally shot by his companion, Brown. The insurance companies rejected the claim based upon declarations made by Brown that Hillmon and he had in fact murdered a Mr. Walters, whom they met along the way, and attempted to pass Walter's body off as Hillmon's in an attempt to defraud the insurance companies. In support of this defense, Mutual (D) attempted to admit into evidence certain letters written by Walters to different members of his family, which placed him in geographic proximity to Hillmon and Brown and mentioned that Walters would be accompanying Hillmon. Mrs. Hillmon (P) objected to the admission of such letters into evidence as inadmissible hearsay. The letters were ruled inadmissible, and a verdict for Mrs. Hillmon (P) was entered. Mutual (D) and the other carriers appealed.

ISSUE: May a party's intentions, when such are distinct and material facts in a chain of circumstances, be proved by contemporaneous oral or written declarations of that party?

HOLDING AND DECISION: (Gray, J.) Yes. Whenever the intentions of a party are themselves a distinct and material fact in a chain of circumstances, they may be proved by contemporaneous oral or written declarations of the party. The letters in question were competent evidence that shortly before the time when Walters went away he had the intention of going, and of going with Hillmon, and that he was in fact the person whose body was offered as the decedent. Thus, the mental feelings of Walters were material in the case with regard to his intention to accompany Hillmon. There was no other way of showing those intentions due to Walters' death; however, they were just as competent as if he had testified to them himself. The letters can be regarded as verbal acts and are as competent as any other testimony due to their relevance. Whether or not they are true or false is a question for the jury. As a result, the two letters involved were competent evidence of Walters' intention at the time of writing them, which was a material fact bearing upon the question in controversy. Reversed and remanded.

EDITOR'S ANALYSIS: It is clear that the letters written in this case could have been excluded under the hearsay rule. They were clearly out-of-court statements offered for their truth. However, they fell within the subsequent-conduct exception recognized by some jurisdictions. The use of the letters was not allowed as independent evidence of Walters' death by Hillmon. However, they were competent as corroborating evidence. The case does not specifically elucidate the other evidence presented by the carriers to determine that Walters was, in fact, the decedent, but it is made clear by the court that the letters were merely corroborating evidence and if offered on their own might not have been considered competent. This is a relatively broad application of an exception to the hearsay rule. Impacting upon this is the indices of the reliability inherent in the letters. There would not appear to have been any alternative motive behind the creation of such letters, and, therefore, the court made a determination that the reliability was high enough to allow them into evidence.

QUICKNOTES

HEARSAY RULE - Rule that an out-of-court statement made by a person, other than the witness testifying at trial and that is offered in order to prove the truth of the matter asserted, is inadmissible.

MATERIAL FACT - A fact without the existence of which a contract would not have been entered.

UNITED STATES v. PHEASTER
Government (P) v. Criminals (D)
544 F.2d 353 (9th Cir. 1976).

NATURE OF CASE: Appeal from various criminal convictions including conspiracy.

FACT SUMMARY: Inciso (D) claimed that it was error for the trial court to have admitted into evidence statements of intention made by the party that he and others, including Pheaster (D), had allegedly conspired to kidnap.

CONCISE RULE OF LAW: Hearsay evidence of statements in which the declarant has stated his intention to do something with another person are admissible under the state of mind exception to the hearsay rule to show that he intended to do it, from which the trier of fact may draw the inference that he carried out his intention and did it.

FACTS: Inciso (D), Pheaster (D), and others were allegedly part of a plot to kidnap and hold for ransom Larry Adell, the 16-year-old son of a Palm Springs multi-millionaire. Larry disappeared forever after leaving his friends at a table at a local restaurant known as Sambo's North, telling them he was going to meet Angelo and he'd be right back. Earlier that day, he had told his girlfriend that he was going to meet Angelo at Sambo's North at 9:30 that night to pick up a pound of marijuana Angelo had promised him for free. She had been with Larry another time when he met a man named Angelo. At trial she identified Inciso (D) as that man. Inciso (D) objected to the introduction of this testimony concerning the statements Larry made to others. The Government (P) insisted it was admissible under the Hillmon doctrine to show Larry's state of mind and thus prove by inference that he acted in accordance with his intention to meet Angelo and did meet him.

ISSUE: Does the Hillmon doctrine permit hearsay evidence of statement by a declarant that he intended to do something with another person to be admitted to show that the declarant had the intention to do it thus permitting the trier of fact to infer that he carried out his intention and did it?

HOLDING AND DECISION: (Renfrew, J.) Yes. The Hillmon doctrine is a particular species of the "state of mind" exception to the general rule that hearsay evidence is inadmissible. Under the Hillmon doctrine, which takes its name from a famous Supreme Court decision, the state of mind of the declarant is used inferentially to prove other matters which are in issue. It does not require that the state of mind of the declarant be an actual issue in the case. Stated simply, the doctrine provides that when the performance of a particular act by an individual is an issue in a case, his intention (state of mind) to perform that act may be shown. From that intention, the trier of fact may draw the inference that the person carried out his intention and performed the act. Within this conceptual framework, hearsay evidence of statements by the person which tend to show his intention is deemed admissible under the state of mind exception. Inciso's (D) objection concerns application of this doctrine to situations in which the declarant has stated his intention to do something with another person, and the issue is whether he did so. When hearsay evidence concerns the declarant's statement of his intention to do something with another person, the Hillmon doctrine requires that the trier of fact infer from the state of mind of the declarant the probability of a particular act not only by the declarant but also by the other person. Several objections can be raised against a doctrine that would allow such an inference to be made. First, it is an unreliable inference. More importantly, however, such an inference is inconsistent with the state of mind exception. Part of the statement that is admitted has nothing to do with the declarant's state of mind. If Larry's friends had testified that he said "Angelo is going to be in the parking lot of Sambo's North tonight with a pound of grass," no state of mind exception or any other exception to the hearsay rule would be available. Yet, this is in effect at least half of what the testimony did attribute to Larry. Despite the theoretical awkwardness associated with the application of the Hillmon doctrine to facts such as those in this case, the authority in favor of such an application is impressive and must be followed. Therefore, although this court recognizes the force of the objection to the application of the Hillmon doctrine in the instant case, it cannot conclude that the district court erred in permitting the testimony concerning Larry Adell's statements.

EDITOR'S ANALYSIS: Although the new Federal Rules of Evidence were not in force when this case came to trial, both the Advisory Committee on the Proposed Rules and the House Committee on the Judiciary specifically addressed the Hillmon doctrine in making statements concerning Rule 803(3), which codifies the state of mind exception to the hearsay rule but does not provide a direct statement of the Hillmon doctrine. The language they used indicates that both bodies perceived the then-prevailing common law view to be that the Hillmon doctrine could be applied in cases where the hearsay statement of intent by a declarant was admitted to prove he did something with another person. However, the Notes of the House Committee stated its intention that the Rule be construed to limit the Hillmon doctrine "so as to render statements of intent by a declarant admissible only to prove his future conduct, not the future conduct of another person." This is contrary to the view which the Advisory Committee obviously had of the effect of Rule 803(3) on the Hillmon doctrine. It stated, "(t)he rule of Mutual Life Ins. Co. v. Hillmon . . . allowing evidence of intention as tending to prove the doing of the act intended is, of course, left undisturbed." Note to Paragraph (3), 28 U.S.C.A. at 585.

BLAKE v. STATE

Stepfather (D) v. State (P)

Wy. Sup. Ct., 933 P.2d 474 (1997).

NATURE OF CASE: Appeal from conviction of second degree sexual assault.

FACT SUMMARY: Blake (D) appealed from his conviction of two counts of second-degree sexual assault of his sixteen-year-old stepdaughter.

CONCISE RULE OF LAW: A statement by a child victim to a medical professional is admissible in situations involving physical or sexual abuse of the child.

FACTS: An investigator from the Department of Family Services (DFS) and an officer from the sheriff's office interviewed the victim, a sixteen-year-old girl, at the local high school in response to a report of sexual abuse. After the interview she was transferred to the hospital emergency room for an examination, during which she told the doctor she had been forcibly subjected to sexual intercourse by her stepfather, Blake (D), several times. The victim was not called to the stand at trial. Instead the State (P) relied upon Blake's (D) typed confession, and the testimony of the doctor, the DFS investigator and the officer. The jury convicted Blake (D) of two counts of second-degree sexual assault and Blake (D) appealed.

ISSUE: Is a statement by a child victim to a medical professional admissible in situations involving physical or sexual abuse of the child?

HOLDING AND DECISION: (Lehman, J.) Yes. A statement by a child victim to a medical professional is admissible in situations involving physical or sexual abuse of the child. In order to admit statements of identity, a two-part test must be satisfied in order to establish the proper foundation under *United States v. Renville*, 779 F.2d 430 (8th Cir. 1985). First the declarant's motive in making the statement must be consistent with the purposes of promoting treatment or diagnosis. Second, the content of the statement must be reasonably relied upon by the physician in rendering the treatment or making the diagnosis. Here the State (P) satisfied the Renville test and laid the proper foundation. The doctor examined the victim as a result of allegations of sexual abuse. In such sexual assault cases the doctor is required to take a history of the patient regarding what happened in order to ascertain the patient's emotional state and to properly collect specimens and render proper medical treatment. Blake (D) argued that this case was distinguishable since the victim was seventeen at the time of trial and her statements lacked the credibility of a younger victim. This argument is without merit. The child's age is a factor to be considered in determining the weight of the evidence, not in its

admissibility. Blake (D) had an opportunity to attack the victim's credibility and failed to do so. Affirmed.

EDITOR'S ANALYSIS: The rule is that statements regarding fault or identity are generally not admissible at trial. The court noted that the statutory exception for statements of child victims to treating physicians was created in order to accommodate for the unique problem of child abuse and to provide proper treatment and diagnosis for such victims.

NOTES:

OHIO v. SCOTT
State (P) v. Convicted shooter (D)
Ohio Sup. Ct., 285 N.E.2d 344 (1972).

NATURE OF CASE: Appeal from criminal convictions.

FACT SUMMARY: Scott (D) objected to the introduction at his criminal trial of a witness' prior written statement to the police as a record of past recollection.

CONCISE RULE OF LAW: The prior recorded statement of a witness in a criminal trial can be admitted under the exception to the hearsay rule for records of "past recollection recorded," and such does not violate the defendant's Sixth Amendment right of confrontation.

FACTS: Scott (D) was convicted of shooting at Williard Lee with intent to kill, wound, or maim, and for shooting at two police officers. On appeal, he argued that the trial court had acted improperly in admitting into evidence the statement of a witness who testified that her memory was better at the time she gave the written and signed statement to the police than it was at the time of trial. Scott (D) maintained the rule of "past recollection recorded" had not been recognized in Ohio, and that employing it in a criminal case deprived the defendant of his Sixth Amendment right of confrontation, including the opportunity of cross-examination. The appellate court affirmed the conviction, and Scott (D) took his arguments to the Supreme Court of Ohio.

ISSUE: Does applying the "past recollection recorded" exception to the hearsay rule so as to admit the prior recorded statement of a witness in a criminal trial violate the Sixth Amendment?

HOLDING AND DECISION: (Leach, J.) No. A defendant's Sixth Amendment rights are not violated by admitting into evidence the prior recorded statement of a witness in a criminal trial under the exception to the hearsay rule for records of "past recollection recorded." As long as the declarant is testifying as a witness, the defendant has the opportunity to conduct a full and effective cross-examination at the time of trial. In this case, the recorded statement consisted of facts of which the witness had firsthand knowledge; it was the original memorandum made near the time of the event while the witness had a clear and accurate memory of it; the witness lacked a present recollection of the exact words Scott (D) had used; and the witness stated that the memorandum was accurate. Thus, all conditions for admissibility were met. Affirmed.

DISSENT: (Corrigan, J.) Aside from the danger that a jury will place too much weight on a written statement, the witness did not testify that she had no present memory of the events recorded therein.

EDITOR'S ANALYSIS: Under the traditional approach, such records of past recollection would not be admissible if examining them could refresh the witness' recollection. Courts are split as to whether any recollection at all is sufficient or whether it must be sufficient to enable the witness to testify fully and accurately, a standard which is gaining in popularity.

QUICKNOTES
FED. R. EVID. 803 - Federal Rule of Evidence setting forth certain exceptions to the hearsay rule, including present sense impressions, excited utterances, present state of mind, statements for medical diagnosis, past recollection recorded, etc.

NOTES:

PETROCELLI v. GALLISON
Patient (P) v. Surgeon (D)
679 F.2d 286 (1st Cir. 1982).

NATURE OF CASE: Appeal of denial of damages for medical malpractice.

FACT SUMMARY: A trial court excluded from evidence a passage from a hospital record because the source of the information contained therein was uncertain.

CONCISE RULE OF LAW: For a portion of a business record to be admissible, the source of the information contained therein must be known.

FACTS: Gallison (D) operated on Petrocelli (P) for a hernia. Petrocelli (P) was afforded no pain relief, and several months later a Dr. Schwartz performed a second procedure, which was also unsuccessful. A third operation proved necessary. Petrocelli (P) sued Gallison (D) for malpractice. An important issue was whether Gallison (D) had inadvertently severed a certain nerve. At trial, Petrocelli attempted to introduce a passage from the operative report related to the second procedure which indicated that the nerve had, in fact, been severed in the original procedure. The source of this information was unknown. The trial court excluded the report. The jury rendered a defense verdict, and Petrocelli (P) appealed.

ISSUE: For a portion of a business record to be admissible, must the source of the information contained therein be known?

HOLDING AND DECISION: (Campbell, J.) Yes. For a portion of a business record to be admissible, the source of the information contained therein must be known. For the business record exception to the hearsay rule to be applicable, it must be demonstrable that the information contained in the record be transmitted by a person with knowledge of the information, and be done in the usual course of business. When a record is completely devoid of any indication as to the source of the information, it cannot be shown that the information therein was, in fact, transmitted by a knowledgeable person. Here, no indication of the source of the information can be found. It is quite likely that the information can be found. It is quite likely that the information came from Petrocelli (P) himself, an individual unqualified to make such an assertion. It was within the trial court's discretion to exclude the evidence. Affirmed.

EDITOR'S ANALYSIS: It would have seemed fairly certain that the evidence came from either the doctors or the Petrocellis (P). Had it come from the doctors, the hearsay exception at issue would have been available. The court discussed whether this issue should have gone to the jury. It concluded that it should not have, as this was within the province of the court under Fed. R. Evid. 104(a).

QUICKNOTES

BUSINESS RECORD - A record made as a part of routine procedure. Admissible as an exception to the hearsay rule.

FED. R. EVID. 104 - Permits a court to consider all nonprivileged matters, whether independently admissible or not, when determining preliminary issues of admissibility.

NOTES:

NORCON, INC. v. KOTOWSKI
Employer (D) v. Employee (P)
Alaska Sup. Ct., 971 P.2d 158 (1999).

NATURE OF CASE: Sexual harassment suit.

FACT SUMMARY: Norcon (D) appealed from a jury verdict in favor of Kotowski (P) in a sexual harassment suit on the basis that the lower court improperly admitted a three-page, handwritten memo under the official business records exception to the hearsay rule.

CONCISE RULE OF LAW: Information that is otherwise hearsay may be admissible under the ordinary business records exception, so long as all of the persons furnishing the information to be recorded are acting in the regular course of business.

FACTS: Kotowski (P) worked on the cleanup of the Exxon Valdez oil spill. Veco, the general contractor, and Norcon (D), a subcontractor, had strict rules against alcohol consumption by person working on the project or living in company housing. Kotowski (P) told Savell, the Exxon executive in charge, that Posehn, Norcon's (D) foreman, was sexually harassing her, that he had invited her to his room that evening and that he expected alcohol to be consumed. Savell gave her a tape recorder and a note stating she had been assigned to help gather information related to drug and/or alcohol abuse, and that she had amnesty from prosecution and termination of her employment. Kotowski (P) was later questioned regarding the party at Posehn's room. Both Posehn and Kotowski (P) were fired. The jury found Norcon (D) liable for sexual harassment and negligent infliction of emotional distress. Kotowski (P) offered into evidence a three-page, handwritten memo summarizing information gathered by a security investigator regarding Posehn. The memo stated that Posehn had many female visitors in his room and that he used the consumption of alcoholic beverages as a "springboard" for sexual activity with female subordinates. The memo also stated that Posehn would do favors for female employees in exchange for sexual activity. Norcon (D) objected to the admission of the memo on the basis that it was inadmissible hearsay. Kotowski (P) argued that the memo was admissible under the official business records exception. Norcon (D) contested that argument on the basis that the report contained hearsay statements of others. The superior court admitted the memo under the exception. Norcon (D) appealed.

ISSUE: May information that is otherwise hearsay be admissible under the ordinary business records exception, so long as all of the persons furnishing the information to be recorded are acting in the regular course of business?

HOLDING AND DECISION: (Matthews, J.) Yes. Information that is otherwise hearsay may be admissible under the ordinary

business records exception, so long as all of the persons furnishing the information to be recorded are acting in the regular course of business. Norcon (D) objected to the memo here on the basis that the memo consisted of double and triple hearsay of the informants who provided the information contained in the memo. Norcon (D) further argued that even if the memo was prepared in the regular course of business, there was no evidence the informants were acting in the regular course of their business. Kotowski (P) argued that the informants had business reasons, as employees of Norcon (D), to provide accurate and true statements. Moreover, Kotowski (P) argued such statements should not be treated as hearsay but rather as admissions of a party-opponent. This argument has merit. The lower court did not err by admitting the memo.

EDITOR'S ANALYSIS: The official business records exception to the hearsay rule is satisfied if all of the following requirements are met: (1) the record is one that is regularly kept in the course of regular business; (2) the source of the information is a person who has personal knowledge of the information stated therein; (3) the information was collected and recorded at a time contemporaneous with the activity observed; and (4) proper foundation is laid by the custodian of the records or another similarly qualified witness.

NOTES:

BAKER v. ELCONA HOMES CORP.

Automobile passenger (P) v. Employee truck driver (D)
588 F.2d 551 (6th Cir. 1978), cert. denied, 441 U.S. 933 (1979).

NATURE OF CASE: Action for damages for negligence.

FACT SUMMARY: Baker (P), who sued to recover damages for a car accident with a truck driven by an Elcona (D) employee, objected to the introduction of a police accident report into evidence.

CONCISE RULE OF LAW: When they result from an investigation made pursuant to authority granted by law, factual findings (including evaluations and opinions) in public records and reports are admissible unless the sources of information or other circumstances indicate lack of trustworthiness.

FACTS: A police accident report was put into evidence when Baker (P) brought a negligence suit to recover damages from Elcona (D) for an accident between one of its truck drivers and the car in which she was riding. The reports contained the officer's opinion that the car had failed to yield the right of way and stated it had "apparently" entered the intersection against a red light. It also contained a statement which the truck driver gave to the officer. On appeal from a verdict for Elcona (D), Baker (P) argued these were not the type of "factual findings" admissible under the exception to the hearsay rule for official written statements in Federal Rule of Evidence 803(8).

ISSUE: Are evaluations and opinions in public records and reports admissible into evidence?

HOLDING AND DECISION: (Engel, J.) Yes. Fed. R. Evid. 803(8) provides that public records can be admitted into evidence under an exception to the hearsay rule. It specifically mentions that the factual findings therein (a term which includes evaluations and opinions) are admissible in civil proceedings and against the government in criminal proceedings unless the sources of information or their circumstances indicate lack of trustworthiness. The four factors to be considered in making that determination are: (1) the timeliness of the investigation; (2) the special skill of or experience of the official; (3) whether a hearing was held on the level at which the investigation was conducted; and (4) possible motivational problems. In this case, they point to the trustworthiness of the objected-to opinions and evaluations in the police report. As to the presence of a statement by the truck driver, it is not hearsay because it is a statement consistent with his testimony and offered to rebut the charge that he recently fabricated his story. Admission of the evidence objected to was entirely proper. Affirmed.

EDITOR'S ANALYSIS: The common-law requirement that the official making the report have firsthand knowledge of those things he records prevented expansion of the official written statements exception to the hearsay rule. However, the Federal Rules of Evidence adopted the less stringent rule of admissibility cited in this case. The Uniform Rules of Evidence have opted for an even broader rule.

QUICKNOTES

FED. R. EVID. 803 - Federal Rule of Evidence setting forth certain exceptions to the hearsay rule, including present sense impressions, excited utterances, present state of mind, statements for medical diagnosis, past recollection recorded, etc.

NOTES:

UNITED STATES v. OATES
Government (P) v. Convicted drug possessor (D)
560 F.2d 45 (2d Cir. 1977).

NATURE OF CASE: Appeal from a conviction for possession of narcotics.

FACT SUMMARY: Oates (D) contended the trial court erred in allowing into evidence a written report identifying as heroin a substance seized in his possession.

CONCISE RULE OF LAW: In criminal cases, reports of public agencies setting forth factual findings resulting from investigations made pursuant to authority granted by law are inadmissible hearsay and not subject to any exception if the reports are sought to be introduced against the accused.

FACTS: Oates (D) was arrested for possession of heroin. He was found with a packet of a certain white powdery substance which was sent to Milton Weinberg, a retired United States Custom Service chemist, for analysis. Weinberg prepared a worksheet which detailed the process by which he analyzed the substance and included his conclusion that the substance was heroin. On the date of trial, however, Weinberg became ill and was unable to testify. The Government (P) produced a Shirley Harrington, who was identified as another Customs chemist who was acquainted with the regular practices and procedures employed by both the Government (P) and by Weinberg in analyzing such substances. She testified that she had herself conducted the tests on other cases, that she had testified many times before on such matters, and that although she did not know Weinberg personally, she did recognize his handwriting and she could ascertain from the report the steps Weinberg had taken in analyzing the substance. The court admitted the worksheet, and Oates (D) was convicted. Oates (D) appealed, contending the report was inadmissible hearsay.

ISSUE: Are reports of public agencies, setting forth factual findings resulting from investigations made pursuant to authority granted by law, inadmissible hearsay and not subject to any exception if such reports are sought to be introduced against the accused?

HOLDING AND DECISION: (Waterman, J.) Yes. In criminal cases, reports of public agencies setting forth factual findings resulting from investigations made pursuant to authority granted by law do not satisfy the standards of any hearsay exception if those reports are sought to be introduced against the accused. Fed. R. Evid. 803(8) clearly establishes that when such reports are used against an accused criminal they are not shielded from the hearsay rule. The factual finding in the case was, of course, the result of the procedure of analysis employed by Weinberg. This gathering of facts was an out-of-court statement offered for proof and, therefore, subject to the hearsay rule. Rule 803 specifically excludes such evidence from the business records and/or public records exception to the hearsay rule. The reason for this is that it deprives the criminal defendant of his right to confrontation under the Constitution. The defendant is not represented at the time these factual findings are recorded, and, therefore, he is not given the ability to confront the witness nor cross-examine him. Further, the trier of fact is deprived of this opportunity to evaluate the reliability and believability of the witness when the recordings are made. As a result, it was error to admit the report, and the conviction must be overturned.

EDITOR'S ANALYSIS: The court also indicated that it felt the report could not come in for a separate reason. Under Fed. R. Evid. 803(8)(B), matters observed by police officers and other law enforcement personnel are, likewise, not protected from the hearsay rule by the public records exception. Mr. Weinberg was employed by the prosecution to analyze the substance. Thus, he could be referred to as "other law enforcement personnel." The law enforcement personnel clearly have a motivation to structure their findings to bolster the law enforcement effort behind convicting the accused. Thus, there is not a requisite level of reliability in these recordings to allow them to fall within the exception to the hearsay rule. It is clear, however, that if the hearsay evidence is offered for a purpose other than against the accused, then they may, in fact, fall within the hearsay exception. It is hard to determine within the criminal context what relevance such evidence would have, unless it were being offered against the accused. Thus, in criminal investigations Fed. R. Evid. 803 is a very limiting rule.

QUICKNOTES

FED. R. EVID. 803 - Federal Rule of Evidence setting forth certain exceptions to the hearsay rule, including present sense impressions, excited utterances, present state of mind, statements for medical diagnosis, past recollection recorded, etc.

NOTES:

BARBER v. PAGE
Convicted robber (D) v. Government (P)
390 U.S. 719 (1968).

NATURE OF CASE: Appeal from a conviction for armed robbery.

FACT SUMMARY: Barber (D) contended the trial court erred in admitting into evidence prior testimony of a co-defendant inculpating him of the crime over his objections which deprived him of his right to confrontation.

CONCISE RULE OF LAW: A witness is not unavailable for purposes of the prior testimony exception to the confrontation requirement unless the prosecutorial authorities have made a good faith effort to obtain his presence at trial.

FACTS: Barber (D) and Woods were jointly charged with armed robbery. At the preliminary hearing both were represented by the same counsel. Woods agreed to waive his privilege against self incrimination, and his counsel withdrew as his attorney. That counsel, however, continued to represent Barber (D). Woods made incriminating statements against himself and Barber at the preliminary hearing. Barber's (D) counsel did not cross-examine Woods at the preliminary hearing; however, an attorney for another co-defendant did. At the time of trial, Woods was incarcerated in a federal penitentiary outside the jurisdiction of the court. The prosecution attempted to admit into evidence the transcript of the preliminary hearing which recorded Woods' testimony, arguing that he was unavailable to testify because he was outside the jurisdiction. They represented to the court that they had not actually inquired of federal authorities whether or not Woods could have been brought to the jurisdiction, explaining that because such a decision on the part of federal authorities would have been discretionary they did not feel that they were required to actually attempt to bring Woods to the court. Barber (D) objected to the admission of such evidence on the basis that it deprived him of his right to confrontation. The court allowed the evidence, and Barber (D) was convicted. He sought federal habeas corpus relief, which was denied. The United States Supreme Court granted certiorari.

ISSUE: Is a witness unavailable for purposes of the prior testimony exception to the confrontation requirement only if the prosecutorial authorities have made a good faith effort to obtain his presence at trial?

HOLDING AND DECISION: (Marshall, J.) Yes. A witness is not unavailable for purposes of the prior testimony exception to the confrontation requirement unless the prosecutorial authorities have made a good faith effort to obtain his presence at trial. Because of the clearly increased cooperation between the federal

and state governments, it was unconscionable for the prosecutorial authorities to make no attempt to bring Woods to Barber's trial. Their failure to exercise even minimal efforts to bring the witness to the trial eliminated the necessity requirement of using the preliminary hearing transcript. It is this necessity requirement which underlies the rationale for the exception to the confrontation clause upon which the government relied. Because this necessity was absence, the use of the preliminary hearing transcript was error and the conviction must be overturned.

EDITOR'S ANALYSIS: The government attempted to argue that Barber (D) had an opportunity to cross-examine Woods at the preliminary hearing, and his failure to do so waived his ability to assert the confrontation defense. However, the Court recognized that there are different motivations at a preliminary hearing than there are at trial. The purpose of the preliminary hearing is merely to establish whether or not there is probable cause to bind the defendant over for trial. Thus, whether or not the decision is to cross-examine or not is made upon different grounds than if the witness were present at trial. Depriving the defendant of his right to cross-examine merely because he failed to do so at the preliminary hearing would clearly infringe upon his rights unfairly. The Court concludes that while actual unavailability need not be shown, at least a good faith effort must be made to produce the actual witness at trial.

QUICKNOTES

CONFRONTATION CLAUSE - A provision in the Sixth Amendment to the United States Constitution that an accused in a criminal action has the right to confront the witnesses against him, including the right to attend the trial and to cross-examine witnesses called on behalf of the prosecution.

LLOYD v. AMERICAN EXPORT LINES, INC.
Seaman (P) v. Shipping company (D)
580 F.2d 1179, cert. denied, 439 U.S. 969 (3d Cir. 1978).

NATURE OF CASE: Counterclaim for damages for negligence and unseaworthiness.

FACT SUMMARY: In defending against a counterclaim brought by Alvarez (D), Export (D) sought to introduce into evidence testimony that Lloyd (P) (who was unavailable) had given at a Coast Guard hearing regarding the fight between himself and Alvarez (D) aboard one of Export's (D) ships.

CONCISE RULE OF LAW: The prior testimony of an unavailable witness is admissible under Fed. R. Evid. 804(b)(1) if the party against whom it is offered or a "predecessor in interest" had the "opportunity and similar motive to develop the testimony by direct, cross or redirect examination."

FACTS: There was a fight between two crew members, Lloyd (P) and Alvarez (D), aboard one of Export's (D) ships. Lloyd (P) sued Export (D), alleging negligence and unseaworthiness. Export (D) joined Alvarez (D) as a third-party defendant, and Alvarez then counterclaimed against Export (D), alleging negligence and unseaworthiness (based on Export's (D) supposed failure to use reasonable precautions to safeguard him from one it knew to have dangerous propensities, i.e., Lloyd (P)). Lloyd's (P) case was dismissed when he repeatedly failed to show up for pretrial depositions and when his case was called for trial. Alvarez (D) proceeded with his counterclaim, testifying to his version of the fight that had occurred between himself and Lloyd (P). The trial court did not permit Export (D) to introduce into evidence Lloyd's (P) prior testimony at a Coast Guard hearing that had been held to determine whether his merchant mariner's document should have been suspended or revoked on the basis of charges of misconduct brought against him for the fight with Alvarez (D). That testimony contained Lloyd's (P) quite different account of the fight that had occurred. At that hearing, both Lloyd (P) and Alvarez (D) were represented by counsel and testified under oath. On appeal, Export (D) argued that the trial court had erred in ruling that this prior testimony was not admissible under Fed. R. Evid. 804(b)(1), which renders admissible the prior testimony of an unavailable witness if the party against whom it is offered or a "predecessor in interest" had the "opportunity and similar motive to develop the testimony by direct, cross or redirect examination."

ISSUE: If a witness is unavailable, does Fed. R. Evid. 804(b)(1) make his prior testimony admissible if the party against whom it is offered or a "predecessor in interest" had the "opportunity and similar motive to develop the testimony by direct, cross or redirect examination?"

HOLDING AND DECISION: (Aldisert, J.) Yes. Under Fed. R. Evid. 804(b)(1), the prior testimony of a witness who is "unavailable" is admissible if the party against whom it is offered or a "predecessor in interest" had the "opportunity and similar motive to develop the testimony by direct, cross or redirect examination." In this case, it is clear that the proponent of Lloyd's (P) statement was unable to procure his attendance by process or other reasonable means and that he must thus be considered to have been "unavailable." As to whether Export (D) can be considered a "predecessor in interest" of Lloyd (D), that is a more difficult question. Congress did not define that phrase, leaving it up to the courts to interpret it. As originally submitted by the Supreme Court, Rule 804(b)(1) would have allowed prior testimony of an unavailable witness to be received in evidence if the party against whom it was offered, or a person with "motive and interest similar," had an opportunity to examine the witness. The change in wording that occurred thereafter to that which is now set forth in Rule 804(b)(1) did not signal a return to the common law approach to former testimony—which required privity or a common property interest between the parties. With that in mind, this court is satisfied that there was a sufficient community of interest shared by the Coast Guard in its hearing and Alvarez (D) in the subsequent civil trial to satisfy Rule 804(b)(1). The Coast Guard investigating officer attempted to establish at the Coast Guard hearing what Alvarez (D) attempted to establish at the later trial: Lloyd's (P) intoxication, his role as the aggressor, and his prior hostility toward Alvarez (D). While the result sought in the two proceedings differed, the basic interest advanced by both was that of determining culpability and, if appropriate, exacting a penalty for the same condemned behavior thought to have occurred. Under the circumstances, this court is satisfied that there existed sufficient "opportunity and similar motive (for the Coast Guard investigating officer) to develop (Lloyd's) testimony" at the former hearing to justify its admission against Alvarez (D) at the later trial. It is this court's belief that Congress intended that when a party in a former suit had a like motive to cross-examine regarding the same matters as the present party would have and had an adequate opportunity to do so, the testimony thus procured in that former suit is admissible against the present party because the previous party was, in the final analysis, a predecessor in interest to the present party.

CONCURRENCE: (Stern, J.) While I agree with the result, I cannot agree with the analysis. I would hold that the prior testimony is admissible under the catch-all exception to the

Continued on next page.

hearsay rule, 804(b)(5), and not under 804(b)(1). Under the majority's approach, it is sufficient that the Coast Guard investigator and Alvarez (D) shared a community of interest, which the majority seems to think means nothing more than similarity of interest or similarity of motive. But similar motive is a separate prerequisite to admissibility under 804(b)(1), and thus the majority's analysis which reads "predecessor in interest" to mean nothing more than person with "similar motive" eliminates the predecessor in interest requirement entirely. It seems clear that the phrase "predecessor in interest" is a term of art having a narrow, substantive law sense that historically requires it to be defined in terms of a privity relationship. No such relationship existed in this case. While the interests of Alvarez (D) and the Coast Guard may overlap, they do not coincide. The Coast Guard investigating officer was under no duty to advance every arguable issue against Lloyd (P) in vindication of Alvarez's (D) interests. He simply did not represent Alvarez (D).

EDITOR'S ANALYSIS: Just precisely when a witness is "unavailable" so that his prior testimony may be admissible is a problem that has plagued the courts. While some have held that a witness' loss of memory of the relevant matters does not render him "unavailable," the general consensus is that it does; so too does his refusal to testify.

NOTES:

WILLIAMSON v. UNITED STATES
Convicted drug offender (D) v. Government (P)
512 U.S. 594 (1994).

NATURE OF CASE: Appeal from conviction of possession of cocaine with intent to distribute, conspiracy to possess cocaine with intent to distribute, and traveling interstate to promote the distribution of cocaine.

FACT SUMMARY: Williamson (D) contended that the district court erred in allowing the testimony of a DEA agent in court who related arguably self-inculpatory statements made out of court to him by Harris, one of Williamson's (D) employees, regarding the possession and transport of the cocaine.

CONCISE RULE OF LAW: Fed. R. Evid. 804(b)(3) does not allow admission of non-self-inculpatory statements, even if they are made within a broader narrative that is generally self-inculpatory.

FACTS: Harris, an employee of Williamson (D), was stopped by the police while he was driving. The police, after searching the car, found 19 kilograms of cocaine in the car and arrested Harris. After his arrest, Harris was interviewed by telephone by a DEA agent, Walton. Harris told Walton that he had gotten the cocaine from a Cuban, that the cocaine belonged to Williamson (D), and that Harris was delivering it to a particular dumpster for pickup. Shortly thereafter, Walton interviewed Harris personally; Harris then told Walton that he was transporting the cocaine to Atlanta for Williamson (D), that Williamson (D) was traveling ahead of him in another car at the time of the arrest, and that Williamson (D) had apparently seen the police searching Harris' car and had fled. Harris told Walton that he had initially lied about the source of the cocaine because he was afraid of Williamson (D). Harris implicated himself in his statements to Walton but did not want his story to be recorded and refused to sign a written transcript of the statement. Walton later testified that Harris was not promised any reward for cooperating. Williamson (D) was eventually charged and convicted of various drug-related offenses. When Harris was called to testify at Williamson's (D) trial, he refused to do so. The district court then ruled that, under Fed. R. Evid. 804(b)(3), Agent Walton could relate what Harris told him because Harris' statements were against his own interests. Williamson (D) was convicted, and the court of appeals affirmed. On appeal, Williamson (D) argued that both lower courts erred by allowing Walton to testify regarding Harris' out-of-court statements.

ISSUE: Does Fed. R. Evid. 804(b)(3) allow admission of non-self-inculpatory statements, even if they are made within a broader narrative that is generally self-inculpatory?

HOLDING AND DECISION: (O'Connor, J.) No. Fed. R. Evid. 804(b)(3) does not allow admission on non-self-inculpatory statements, even if they are made within a broader narrative that

is generally self-inculpatory. The district court may not just assume, for purposes of Rule 804(b)(3), that a statement is self-inculpatory because it is part of a fuller confession, and this is especially true when the statement implicates someone else. The question under the Rule is always whether the statement was sufficiently against the declarant's penal interest that a reasonable person would not have made the statement unless believing it to be true. This question can only be answered in light of all the surrounding circumstances. In this case, some of Harris' confession would clearly have been admissible under the Rule. For instance, when he said he knew there was cocaine in the car, he forfeited his only defense to the charge of cocaine possession—lack of knowledge. But other parts of his confession, especially those in which he implicated Williamson (D), did little to subject Harris to criminal liability. A reasonable person in Harris' position might think that implicating someone else would decrease his own exposure to criminal liability at sentencing. Nothing in the record shows that the district court or court of appeals inquired whether each of the statements in Harris' confession was truly self-inculpatory. Remanded to the court of appeals to conduct this inquiry.

CONCURRENCE: (Scalia, J.) A declarant's statement is not magically transformed from a statement against penal interest into one that is inadmissible merely because the declarant names another person or implicates a possible codefendant. The relevant inquiry, however—and one that is not furthered by clouding the waters with manufactured categories such as "collateral neutral" and "collateral self-serving"—must always be whether the particular remark at issue (and not the extended narrative) meets the standard set forth in the Rule.

CONCURRENCE: (Ginsburg, J.) An arrested person has "strong incentive to shift blame or downplay his own role" in hope of leniency and a shorter sentence. Hence, none of the statements by Harris fit the exception, "even in part." The remand is justified only to let the government argue that admitting the statement was harmless error.

CONCURRENCE: (Kennedy, J.) Rule 804(b)(3) establishes a hearsay exception for statements against penal, proprietary, pecuniary, and legal interest. The text of the Rule does not tell us whether collateral statements are admissible. The Court resolves this issue by adopting the extreme position that no collateral statements are admissible under the Rule. The Court reaches that conclusion by relying on the "principle behind the Rule" that

Continued on next page.

reasonable people do not make statements against their interest unless they are telling the truth, and reasons that this policy "expressed in the statutory text" simply does not extend to collateral statements. To the contrary, three sources indicate that the Rule allows the admission of some collateral statements: first, the Advisory Committee Note to the Rule establishes that some collateral statements are admissible; second, at common law, collateral statements were admissible, and we can presume that Congress intended the principle and terms used in the Federal Rules of Evidence to be applied as they were at common law; third, absent a textual direction to the contrary, we should assume that Congress intended the penal interest exception for inculpatory statements to have some meaningful effect. The exclusion of collateral statements would cause the exclusion of almost all inculpatory statements.

EDITOR'S ANALYSIS: As indicated by the Court in *Williamson*, Rule 804(b)(3) requires that self-inculpatory statements should be examined in terms of the reasonable person and that the declarant believe the statement to be against interest. In order to analyze whether the declarant truly believes his statement was against interest, the identity of the person to whom the statement was made should be considered. Although the situation wherein a declarant makes his statement to the authorities is the prime example of a statement against interest, if such a statement was made to a trusted friend (who was expected to keep the information secret), it has not necessarily been held that this eliminates the disserving nature of the statement.

NOTES:

STATE v. WEAVER
State (P) v. Caretaker (D)
Iowa Sup. Ct., 554 N.W.2d 240 (1996).

NATURE OF CASE: Appeal from first-degree murder conviction.

FACT SUMMARY: Weaver (D) appealed from her conviction for first-degree murder of eleven-month old Melissa Mathes on the basis of affidavits of several women regarding statements by the child's mother that she hit her head on a coffee table.

CONCISE RULE OF LAW: In making a trustworthiness determination, the court must consider the declarant's propensity to tell the truth, whether the alleged statements were made under oath, assurances of the declarant's personal knowledge, the time lapse between the event and the statement concerning the event, and the motivations of the declarant.

FACTS: Weaver (D) was charged with first degree murder and child endangerment of eleven-month old Melissa Mathes. Weaver (D) picked up Melissa at the Mathes home and later called 911 to report that the child was not breathing. Melissa died of respiratory arrest the following day. An autopsy revealed old and recent injuries consistent with "shaken baby syndrome." After her conviction Weaver (D) moved for a new trial on the basis of affidavits stating that Melissa's mother had said that Weaver (D) did not hurt the child and that the baby had hit her head on a coffee table at their home prior to being placed in Weaver's (D) care. The motion was denied on the basis that the affidavits contained hearsay and did not fall into any exception to the rule. The court of appeals affirmed and the Iowa Supreme Court remanded to consider a seconf motion for a new trial based on three new affidavits of other women regarding statements made by Melissa's mother regarding the baby having hit her head on the coffee table that morning.

ISSUE: In making a trustworthiness determination, what factors must the court consider?

HOLDING AND DECISION: (McGiverin, C.J.) In making a trustworthiness determination, the court must consider the declarant's propensity to tell the truth, whether the alleged statements were made under oath, assurances of the declarant's personal knowledge, the time lapse between the event and the statement concerning the event, and the motivations of the declarant. Additional circumstances to be considered include corroboration, the delclarant's reaffirmation or recanting of the statement, the credibility of the witness and the availability of the declarant for cross-examination. Here the court did not abuse its discretion in ruling the affidavits were admissible hearsay evidence in ruling on the defendant's second motion for a new

trial. The only issue on appeal here is the trustworthiness of the affidavits ands testimony. The district court's factual findings concluded that here the witnesses were credible, the declarant was available to testify, the statements were made in close proximity to the events, the declarant had firsthand knowledge of the information, the statement was unambiguous, voluntary and made to more than one person on separate occasions, and the statement was corroborated by medical evidence. Thus the district court's decision to admit the affidavits was not an abuse of discretion.

EDITOR'S ANALYSIS: This case deals with the catchall exceptions, now found in Fed. R. Evid. 807. The catchall exceptions allow the court to admit evidence that otherwise constitutes hearsay if it meets the requirements of trustworthiness. Here the hearsay evidence was admitted under the catchall exception for the purpose of introducing exonerating facts.

NOTES:

OHIO v. ROBERTS
Government (P) v. Convicted criminal (D)
448 U.S. 56 (1980).

NATURE OF CASE: Appeal from conviction for forgery and receiving stolen property.

FACT SUMMARY: Roberts (D) contended that the trial court denied him his right to confront a witness when it admitted into evidence the witness' testimony in the form of a transcript from the preliminary hearing.

CONCISE RULE OF LAW: The right to confrontation is not violated by the presentation of the transcript testimony where there was an adequate opportunity to cross-examine the witness at the official proceeding where the testimony was given.

FACTS: Roberts (D) was charged with forgery of a check in the name of Bernard Isaacs and possession of stolen credit cards belonging to Isaac's wife, Amy. At the preliminary hearing, Roberts' (D) counsel saw Anita Isaacs, Bernard's daughter, in the hallway and called her to testify. He vigorously attempted to get her to admit that she had given Roberts (D) her father's checkbook, her mother's credit cards and told him he had permission to use them. She denied this, and the prosecution did not question her. Roberts (D) was indicted, and at trial, the prosecution, after showing Anita was unavailable, was allowed to introduce the transcript from the preliminary hearing. He was convicted and appealed, contending the admission of the transcript denied him his right to confrontation. The Ohio Supreme Court reversed, holding the mere opportunity to cross-examine did not satisfy the Confrontation Clause. The State (P) appealed.

ISSUE: Is the right to confrontation violated by the presentation of transcript testimony where there was an adequate opportunity for cross-examination?

HOLDING AND DECISION: (Blackmun, J.) No. The right to confrontation is not violated by the presentation of transcript testimony where there was an adequate opportunity to cross-examine the witness at the official proceeding where the testimony was given. Prior testimony is admissible as an exception to the hearsay rule if it bears adequate indicia of reliability. Anita's testimony was given under oath, and Robert's (D) attorney had an adequate opportunity, through the use of leading questions, to effectively cross-examine her. Therefore, the testimony in fact bore adequate indicia of reliability and was admissible. Reversed.

EDITOR'S ANALYSIS: Because of the fact that the declarant was under oath at the time, prior testimony is admitted as an exception to the hearsay rule. The introduction of this type of evidence requires that the proponent prove its necessity. Such necessity is shown by the declarant's unavailability. This requirement of necessity is in conformance with the framer's objective in creating the Confrontation Clause in the Sixth Amendment.

QUICKNOTES

CONFRONTATION CLAUSE - A provision in the Sixth Amendment to the United States Constitution that an accused in a criminal action has the right to confront the witnesses against him, including the right to attend the trial and to cross-examine witnesses called on behalf of the prosecution.

NOTES:

CRAWFORD v. WASHINGTON
Criminal defendant (D) v. State (P)
U.S. Supreme Court 2004 WL 413301 (2004).

NATURE OF CASE: Appeal from a criminal conviction.

FACT SUMMARY: When the prosecution played the tape-recorded statement of a witness against him at trial, which did not afford the opportunity for cross-examination, Crawford (D) argued he was denied the Sixth Amendment's guarantee of confrontation.

CONCISE RULE OF LAW: Where testimonial statements are at issue, the only indicium of reliability sufficient to satisfy constitutional demands is the one the Constitution actually prescribes: confrontation.

FACTS: Michael Crawford (D) stabbed a man who allegedly tried to rape his wife, Sylvia. At his trial, the prosecution played for the jury Sylvia's tape-recorded statement to the police describing the stabbing, even though Crawford (D) had no opportunity for cross-examination. The jury found Crawford (D) guilty. The Washington Court of Appeals reversed, but the Washington Supreme Court upheld the conviction after determining that Sylvia's statement was reliable. Crawford (D) appealed to the U.S. Supreme Court, contending that the State of Washington's (P) procedure of playing the tape violated the Sixth Amendment's guarantee that in all criminal prosecutions the accused shall enjoy the right to be confronted with the witnesses against him.

ISSUE: Where testimonial statements are at issue, is confrontation the only indicium of reliability sufficient to satisfy constitutional demands?

HOLDING AND DECISION: (Scalia, J.) Yes. Where testimonial statements are at issue, the only indicium of reliability sufficient to satisfy constitutional demands is confrontation. Here, the state admitted Sylvia's testimonial statement against Crawford (D) despite the fact that he had no opportunity to cross-examine her. That alone is sufficient to make out a violation of the Sixth Amendment. This court will not mine the record in search of indicia of reliability. Although where nontestimonial hearsay is at issue, it is wholly consistent with the Framers' design to afford the states flexibility in their development of hearsay law. Where testimonial evidence is at issue, the Sixth Amendment demands what the common law required: unavailability and a prior opportunity for cross-examination. Whatever else the term "testimonial" covers, it applies at a minimum to prior testimony at a preliminary hearing, before a grand jury, or at a former trial, and to police interrogations. These are the modern practices with closest kinship to the abuses at which the Confrontation Clause was directed. The Constitution prescribes the procedure for determining the reliability of testimony in criminal trials, and this Court, no less than the state courts, lacks authority to replace it

with one of our own devising. By replacing categorical constitutional guarantees with open-ended balancing tests, we would do violence to the Framers' design. Reversed and remanded.

EDITOR'S ANALYSIS: In *Crawford*, the Supreme Court makes clear that where testimonial statements are involved in criminal cases, the Framers did not intend to leave the Sixth Amendment's protection to the vagaries of the rules of evidence, much less to amorphous notions of "reliability." Legal authorities and scholars do not acknowledge any general reliability exception to the common law confrontation rule. In this regard, the *Crawford* decision notes that admitting statements simply because they are deemed reliable by a judge is fundamentally at odds with the right of confrontation. While the Sixth Amendment's ultimate goal is to ensure reliability of evidence, it is a procedural rather than a substantive guarantee. It commands, not that evidence be reliable, but that reliability be assessed in a particular manner: by cross-examination.

NOTES:

IDAHO v. WRIGHT
Government (P) v. Convicted child molester (D)
497 U.S. 805 (1990).

NATURE OF CASE: Review of order reversing conviction of child molestation.

FACT SUMMARY: A trial court admitted certain hearsay statements by an alleged child molestation victim, finding that extrinsic evidence corroborated the statements.

CONCISE RULE OF LAW: Extrinsic evidence of the reliability of hearsay statements of an alleged child abuse victim may not be considered by a court in deciding upon the admissibility of the statement.

FACTS: Wright (D) and a companion were accused of sexually molesting her two daughters. During the course of the state's investigation, the younger daughter, three years old, was interviewed by a physician, who elicited certain statements tending to incriminate Wright (D). Wright (D) was charged with molestation of the two children. At trial, the younger daughter did not testify, but the court admitted, over Wright's (D) hearsay and Confrontation Clause objections, the statements of the child. The court admitted the statements under Idaho's residual hearsay rule of evidence, which permitted introduction of hearsay evidence having substantial indicia of reliability. The court found, in light of extrinsic evidence adduced at trial, that there was substantial likelihood of reliability. Wright (D) was convicted. The state supreme court reversed, holding the Confrontation Clause to have been offended. The Supreme Court granted certiorari.

ISSUE: May extrinsic evidence of the reliability of hearsay statements of an alleged child abuse victim be considered by a court in deciding upon the admissibility of the statement?

HOLDING AND DECISION: (O'Connor, J.) No. Extrinsic evidence of the reliability of hearsay statements of an alleged child abuse victim may not be considered by a court in deciding upon the admissibility of the statement. The Confrontation Clause requires that, for a hearsay statement to be admissible, the declarant must be unavailable and have sufficient indicia of reliability that cross-examination would be unlikely to harm its credibility. These indicia of reliability exist either in the situation where a hearsay exception firmly rooted in common law is in issue or where a showing of particularized guarantees of trustworthiness are shown. A residual hearsay exception, such as that invoked here, must of necessity fulfill the second element. Particularized guarantees of trustworthiness relate to the process whereby the statement was given; they must be intrinsic to the statement itself. A court, in ruling on trustworthiness, may not look to extrinsic facts to bolster the credibility of the statement. Here, the trial court did just that. The state supreme court was correct in perceiving this as fatally flawing the trial court's analysis of admissibility. The state supreme court found that, absent the extrinsic evidence, the statement could not be considered reliable and, therefore, properly reversed the trial court. Affirmed.

DISSENT: (Kennedy, J.) Corroborating evidence is quite germane to the reliability of an out-of-court statement and should be used by a court in determining whether a child's out-of-court statements were sufficiently reliable to overcome a hearsay objection.

EDITOR'S ANALYSIS: The state hearsay exception invoked here was analogous to Fed. R. Evid. 804(b)(5). This rule excepts from the hearsay rule statements which, although not falling within a traditional exception, have substantially equivalent guarantees of trustworthiness. However, the procedural obstacles that will be faced by a party wishing to introduce a hearsay statement pursuant to this rule are substantial.

QUICKNOTES

CONFRONTATION CLAUSE - A provision in the Sixth Amendment to the United States Constitution that an accused in a criminal action has the right to confront the witnesses against him, including the right to attend the trial and to cross-examine witnesses called on behalf of the prosecution.

NOTES:

CHAPTER 5
RELEVANCE REVISITED

QUICK REFERENCE RULES OF LAW

1. **Remedial Measures.** Subsequent remedial measure evidence is not generally admissible for impeachment purposes if it is merely offered to contradict a defense witness' testimony. (Tuer v. McDonald)

TUER v. McDONALD

Patient's widow (P) v. Doctor (D)

Md. Ct. of App., 701 A.2d 1101 (1997).

NATURE OF CASE: Medical malpractice suit.

FACT SUMMARY: Mary Tuer (P) brought suit against St. Joseph's Hospital (D) and two surgeons alleging medical malpractice based on their failure to readminister Heparin, an anticoagulant, to her husband after his surgery was postponed, allegedly leading his suffering from cardiac arrest and subsequent death.

CONCISE RULE OF LAW: Subsequent remedial measure evidence is not generally admissible for impeachment purposes if it is merely offered to contradict a defense witness' testimony.

FACTS: Mary Tuer (P) brought a medical malpractice suit against St. Joseph's Hospital (D) and doctors McDonald (D) and Brawley (D) after her husband, Eugene, died of cardiac arrest while awaiting coronary artery bypass graft surgery (CABG). Eugene was admitted to the hospital (D) and scheduled for surgery. He was placed on Atenol and Heparin. Following hospital (D) procedure, the anesthesiologist stopped the Heparin Monday morning so that he would not have an anticoagulant in his system during surgery. Eugene was prepared for surgery but an emergency involving another patient required Eugene's surgery to be postponed. Shortly thereafter Eugene went into cardiac arrest and died the next day. After Eugene's death, the hospital (D) changed its procedure with respect to discontinuing Heparin for patients with stable angina. Heparin is now continued until the patient is taken into the operating room. The defendants made a motion in limine to exclude reference to the change in procedure. Tuer (P) argued that the evidence was admissible since the change was not a remedial measure because the hospital claimed the prior procedure was correct and that she was entitled to prove the change to show that continuing Heparin was "feasible." The trial court rejected the first argument but stated that it would admit the evidence if the hospital (D) denied feasibility.

ISSUE: Is subsequent remedial measure evidence generally admissible for impeachment purposes if it is merely offered to contradict a defense witness' testimony?

HOLDING AND DECISION: (Wilner, J.) No. Subsequent remedial measure evidence is not generally admissible for impeachment purposes if it is merely offered to contradict a defense witness' testimony. Maryland Rule 5-407 exempt evidence of subsequent remedial measures when it is offered to prove feasibility, if feasibility has been controverted. This requires the court to determine what is meant by the term feasibility and whether feasibility was in fact controverted. Jurisdictions are divided in construing the feasibility exception. One view is that the term feasibility should be defined narrowly, excluding evidence of subsequent remedial measures unless the defendant specifically argues the measures were not possible under the prevailing circumstances. This view states that feasibility is not controverted (and subsequent remedial evidence not admissible) if a defendant contend the design or practice was chosen due to its perceived advantage over the alternative design or practice; if the defendant claims the instructions or warnings were adequate and additional or different warnings or instructions could not have been given; or the defendant claims the alternative would not have prevented the type of injury sustained in the present case. The other, more expansive view concludes that "feasible" applies not only to that which is possible that which is capable of being utilized successfully. Here the expert testimony did not suggest that the Heparin could not have been readministered following the postponement of Eugene's surgery; instead they contend there were no signs of renewed unstable angina. McDonald (D) stated that the Heparin was not continued because he regarded it as unsafe is equal to a statement that it was unfeasible. This statement suffices to controvert the feasibility of the measure. Affirmed.

EDITOR'S ANALYSIS: The exclusion of evidence for subsequent remedial measures is based primarily on public policy reasons. The legislature seeks to encourage businesses and persons to adopt improved procedures or designs. If evidence of such improvements were admissible, the fear is that this evidence would lead to a presumption of negligence or admission of guilt with respect to the prior procedure.

NOTES:

CHAPTER 6
COMPETENCY OF WITNESSES

QUICK REFERENCE RULES OF LAW

1. **Competency: The Modern View.** Legal insanity alone will not make a witness incompetent to testify. (United States v. Lightly)

2. **The Oath Requirement.** One may not testify if he refuses to swear to tell the truth. (United States v. Fowler)

3. **The Child Witness.** A young child may testify if he demonstrates an understanding of the concepts of truth and falsehood. (Ricketts v. Delaware)

4. **Previously Hypnotized Witnesses.** A criminal defendant may not be prevented as a matter of law from introducing testimony influenced by hypnosis. (Rock v. Arkansas)

5. **Postverdict Testimony by Jurors.** Juror testimony to the effect that jurors sat while intoxicated is an insufficient basis upon which to grant a new trial. (Tanner v. United States)

UNITED STATES v. LIGHTLY
Government (P) v. Convicted felon (D)
677 F.2d 1027 (4th Cir. 1982).

NATURE OF CASE: Appeal of conviction for assault with intent to commit murder.

FACT SUMMARY: A court did not permit McDuffie to testify at trial because he was legally insane.

CONCISE RULE OF LAW: Legal insanity alone will not make a witness incompetent to testify.

FACTS: Lightly (D) and McDuffie were involved in an incident in which McKinley was seriously injured by repeated stabbings. They were all inmates in the same prison. Lightly (D) was charged with assault with intent to commit murder. McDuffie was not charged, as he was ruled insane and not competent to stand trial. Lightly (D) maintained he had only tried to break up McDuffie's assault upon McKinley. McDuffie was prepared to testify that this was true. The court did not permit McDuffie to testify because of his insanity. Lightly (D) was convicted, and he appealed.

ISSUE: Will legal insanity alone make a witness incompetent to testify?

HOLDING AND DECISION: (Ervin, J.) No. Legal insanity alone will not make a witness incompetent to testify. Every witness is presumed to be competent to testify, unless it can be shown he has no relevant knowledge, cannot recall, or cannot testify truthfully. Legal insanity may indeed result in such a disqualification, but does not automatically do so. The trial court should have conducted an in camera hearing to make this determination. Reversed.

EDITOR'S ANALYSIS: Probably no area of evidence has changed more from the early common law rules than competency. Common law contained many disqualifications, such as marriage, mental illness, religious beliefs, and criminal convictions. These have all been removed.

QUICKNOTES

IN CAMERA - In private chambers.

UNITED STATES v. FOWLER
Government (P) v. Tax protester (D)
605 F.2d 181 (5th Cir. 1979).

NATURE OF CASE: Appeal of conviction for tax evasion.

FACT SUMMARY: Fowler (D), who was charged with tax evasion, was not permitted to testify because he refused to swear to tell the truth.

CONCISE RULE OF LAW: One may not testify if he refuses to swear to tell the truth.

FACTS: Fowler (D), an apparent tax protester, was indicted for tax evasion. At trial, he refused to take the oath to tell the truth. The trial court consequently refused to permit him to testify in his defense. He was convicted, and he appealed.

ISSUE: May one testify if he refuses to swear to tell the truth?

HOLDING AND DECISION: (Gee, J.) No. One may not testify if he refuses to swear to tell the truth. Fed. R. Evid. 603 clearly requires that, before testifying, every witness will swear to tell the truth, on oath or affirmation. Therefore, taking the oath is a precondition to the right to testify. Since Fowler (D) refused to take the oath, the district court properly did not permit him to testify. Affirmed.

EDITOR'S ANALYSIS: The requirement that a witness take an oath generally has been held to go beyond merely reciting the words. A witness generally must understand the import of the words. For this reason, insanity or infancy will usually disqualify a witness if the condition makes it impossible to understand the meaning of the words.

NOTES:

RICKETTS v. DELAWARE
Convicted rapist (D) v. Government (P)
Del. Sup. Ct., 488 A.2d 856 (1985).

NATURE OF CASE: Appeal of conviction for rape.

FACT SUMMARY: A young child was permitted to testify against Ricketts (D) after she demonstrated an understanding of the concepts of truth and falsehood.

CONCISE RULE OF LAW: A young child may testify if he demonstrates an understanding of the concepts of truth and falsehood.

FACTS: Ricketts (D) was accused of raping an acquaintance's five-year-old daughter. At trial, the child was examined by the court and counsel as to her understanding of the concepts of truth and falsehood. While she didn't understand the concept of perjury, she clearly understood the difference between the truth and a lie. The court permitted her to testify. Ricketts (D) was convicted, and he appealed.

ISSUE: May a young child testify if he demonstrates an understanding of the concepts of truth and falsehood?

HOLDING AND DECISION: (Moore, J.) Yes. A young child may testify if he demonstrates an understanding of the concepts of truth and falsehood. Under Delaware evidence rules, anyone is presumed to be competent to testify, provided they take the oath and demonstrate a basic understanding as to its meaning. The mental or moral capacity of the witness goes to credibility, not competency. Here, the child did demonstrate an understanding of the concept of truth, and she was, therefore, competent. Affirmed.

EDITOR'S ANALYSIS: At common law, young children were presumed incompetent to testify. Some jurisdictions still retain vestiges of this. The federal rules, however, have completely jettisoned this. The Delaware rules here were patterned after the federal rules.

QUICKNOTES
COMPETENCY TO TESTIFY - Those qualifications necessary for a witness to give testimony at a trial consistent with the requirements of law.

NOTES:

ROCK v. ARKANSAS
Criminal defendant (D) v. Government (P)
483 U.S. 44 (1987).

NATURE OF CASE: Appeal of conviction for manslaughter.

FACT SUMMARY: Rock (D) was not permitted to testify as to matters in which her recollection had been refreshed by hypnosis.

CONCISE RULE OF LAW: A criminal defendant may not be prevented as a matter of law from introducing testimony influenced by hypnosis.

FACTS: Rock (D) was involved in an altercation with her husband which ended in his death by shooting. Rock (D) claimed to have only a vague memory of what occurred. Through hypnotic trance, she purportedly recalled that her finger was not on the trigger when the gun discharged. Expert examination revealed that the gun did have a propensity to fire at improper times. In response to a motion in limine, the trial court excluded all testimony possibly aided by the hypnosis as unreliable. Rock (D) was convicted. On appeal, the state supreme court laid down a rule that no hypnosis-induced testimony would be admissible in any case, civil or criminal. The U.S. Supreme Court granted review.

ISSUE: May a criminal defendant be prevented as a matter of law from introducing testimony influenced by hypnosis?

HOLDING AND DECISION: (Blackmun, J.) No. A criminal defendant may not be prevented from introducing testimony influenced by hypnosis. One of the most basic rules in our system of criminal justice is that a defendant has an absolute right to testify in his own behalf. This right is implied from provisions of the Fifth, Sixth, and Fourteenth Amendments. A necessary component of this right is the ability of the defendant to "tell his story" in his own words. States have at various times created competency rules based on the notion that the right of the witness to give his testimony is subordinate to the state's interest in guaranteeing reliable evidence. This is not so. A state certainly has an interest in preventing perjury, but where it cannot show that a per se incompetency rule is absolutely necessary, such a rule cannot be condoned. Here, hypnosis as a memory-enhancing device is still largely an unexplored area; it simply cannot be said that testimony gained therefrom is inherently unreliable. While a state can devise rules to enhance its probative value, such as requiring proper credentials by those employing it, the state cannot, on a per se basis, exclude all hypnotically induced testimony. Reversed.

EDITOR'S ANALYSIS: The Arkansas Supreme Court borrowed much of its reasoning from *People v. Shirley*, 31 Cal. 3d 18 (1982). This, one of the first major cases to deal with hypnotically induced testimony, also laid down a broad exclusionary rule.

Unlike in the present case, however, the court there excepted criminal defendants from the ambit of the decision.

QUICKNOTES

IN LIMINE - Motion by one party brought prior to trial to exclude the potential introduction of highly prejudicial evidence.

NOTES:

TANNER v. UNITED STATES
Convicted felon (D) v. Government (P)
483 U.S.107 (1987).

NATURE OF CASE: Review of order denying new trial in criminal prosecution.

FACT SUMMARY: Tanner (D) contended that he was entitled to a new trial because of juror testimony to the effect that several jurors sat while intoxicated.

CONCISE RULE OF LAW: Juror testimony to the effect that jurors sat while intoxicated is an insufficient basis upon which to grant a new trial.

FACTS: Tanner (D) was tried and convicted of mail fraud. Following the trial, two jurors stepped forward and told Tanner's (D) attorney of the use by several jurors of intoxicating substances, namely, beer, wine, marijuana, and cocaine. Based on affidavits executed by the jurors, Tanner moved for a new trial. The district court denied the motion, and the court of appeals affirmed. Tanner (D) petitioned for certiorari to the Supreme Court.

ISSUE: Is juror testimony to the effect that jurors sat while intoxicated a sufficient basis upon which to grant a new trial?

HOLDING AND DECISION: (O'Connor, J.) No. Juror testimony to the effect that jurors sat while intoxicated is an insufficient basis upon which to grant a new trial. By the beginning of the twentieth century, the rule had been clearly established that juror testimony could not be admitted to impeach a verdict. This rule was based on the necessity of ensuring the finality of jury verdicts. To hold otherwise would open up juries to post-verdict probing by the losing party, with the concomitant possibility of verdicts being set aside at any time. It is doubtful if the jury system could survive this. An exception has been recognized: juror testimony regarding improper external influences on a jury may be admitted to impeach a verdict. However, juror intoxication cannot be considered an external influence, as no outside actor is involved. For this reason, the district court properly rejected Tanner's (D) motion for a new trial. Affirmed.

EDITOR'S ANALYSIS: The Court did not address the issue of what the result might be if nonjuror witnesses offered evidence of improper juror conduct. Generally, the rules regarding impeachment of jury verdicts by evidence apart from juror testimony are less rigid than those governing juror testimony. Nonetheless, courts are loath to upset verdicts based on juror misconduct.

NOTES:

CHAPTER 7
DIRECT AND CROSS–EXAMINATION REVISITED

QUICK REFERENCE RULES OF LAW

1. **Exceptions—Leading Questions Allowed.** Anything can be used to refresh a witness' recollection of an event, even a memorandum made by another, and it need not meet the standards applicable to a record of past recollection. (Baker v. State)

2. **Cross-Examining on Witness Preparation Material.** The work product privilege may be waived if such product is used to prepare a witness to testify. (James Julian, Inc. v. Raytheon Co.)

BAKER v. STATE
Convicted felon (D) c. Government (P)
Md. Ct. of App. 371 A.2d 699 (1977).

NATURE OF CASE: Appeal from a conviction for first-degree murder and robbery.

FACT SUMMARY: Baker's (D) counsel was not permitted to use a police report prepared by another officer to refresh the recollection of Officer Bolton while he was on the stand testifying.

CONCISE RULE OF LAW: Anything can be used to refresh a witness' recollection of an event, even a memorandum made by another, and it need not meet the standards applicable to a record of past recollection.

FACTS: Baker (D) was convicted of robbery and murder in the first degree. On appeal therefrom, she argued that the trial judge had erred in refusing her counsel the opportunity to refresh the present recollection of a police officer who was testifying by showing him a report written by a fellow officer. In cross-examining Officer Bolton, Baker's (D) counsel sought to elicit from him the fact that the crime victim confronted Baker (D) and stated that she was not one of the persons who had attacked and robbed him. Officer Bolton had stated he did not remember whom it was the crime victim had so confronted, and Baker's (D) counsel sought to have him look at a police report prepared by another officer to refresh his memory on that point. The judge did not allow it.

ISSUE: Can a memorandum made by another be used to refresh a witness' recollection of an event?

HOLDING AND DECISION: (Moylan, J.) Yes. There is no limit as to what can be used to refresh a witness' recollection of an event; even another's memorandum can be so used. The stimulus that is thus used to revive a witness' dormant memory is not itself received in evidence. Thus, it is not to be confused with documents admitted into evidence as embodiments of past recollections recorded and not subject to the same stringent rules of admission. All that is required is that the stimulus ignite the flash of accurate recall, i.e., that it accomplish the revival which is sought. The stimulus used need not even be in writing. Even if it is a writing, it need not have ever been read by the witness before he sees it at trial nor does the witness have to vouch for it or its accuracy. Under these principles, Baker's (D) counsel should have been allowed to refresh Officer Bolton's present recollection with a fellow officer's report. Reversed and remanded for a new trial.

EDITOR'S ANALYSIS: Whatever memory aid is used to refresh a witness' recollection, it is always subject to inspection by the opposing party, who has the right to show it to the jury. The party seeking to use the memory aid may not submit it to the jury for their inspection, however, unless it constitutes evidence that is otherwise admissible.

NOTES:

JAMES JULIAN, INC. v. RAYTHEON CO.
Company (P) v. Company (D)
93 F.R.D. 138 (D. Del. 1982).

NATURE OF CASE: Motion to compel discovery in a civil proceeding.

FACT SUMMARY: Materials which constituted attorney work product were used to prepare witnesses for testifying.

CONCISE RULE OF LAW: The work product privilege may be waived if such product is used to prepare a witness to testify.

FACTS: In a labor dispute, James Julian, Inc. (P) sought damages and injunctive relief against Raytheon Co. (D) and several individuals. During the course of the litigation, counsel for Julian (P) prepared a binder of documents, some of which it had obtained through discovery, others of which it had obtained through investigation. Counsel used the materials therein to prepare witnesses for deposition testimony. Upon discovering that these materials had been used to prepare the witnesses, counsel for Raytheon (D) demanded production of the binder. Julian (P) refused, citing work product. Raytheon (D) made a motion to compel.

ISSUE: May the work product privilege be waived if such product is used to prepare a witness to testify?

HOLDING AND DECISION: (Schwartz, J.) Yes. The work product privilege may be waived if such product is used to prepare a witness to testify. Federal Rule of Evidence 612 gives an opposing party the right to examine documents used to refresh a witness' recollection or to prepare them to testify. While the rule is unclear as to whether Congress intended it to apply to privileged documents, the majority of courts, when faced with the attorney-client privilege, have held that it would be manifestly unfair to deny an opposing party the right to inspect documents used to prepare a witness, and to make an exception for privileged documents would create an avenue for attorneys to circumvent this principle. These arguments apply with equal force to the work product privilege and for that reason counsel for Raytheon (D) must be permitted to inspect the binder. Motion granted.

EDITOR'S ANALYSIS: Fed. R. Evid. 612, discussed here, constituted a major change from prior law. Prior to its adoption, opposing counsel was permitted to inspect a document used to refresh recollection only if it was used on the stand. The Rule now mandates disclosure if any particular document was used at any time to prepare a witness.

QUICKNOTES

ATTORNEY-CLIENT PRIVILEGE - A doctrine precluding the admission into evidence of confidential communications between an attorney and his client made in the course of obtaining professional assistance.

WORK PRODUCT RULE - A doctrine excluding from discovery work performed by an attorney in preparation of litigation.

NOTES:

CHAPTER 8
IMPEACHMENT OF WITNESSES

QUICK REFERENCE RULES OF LAW

1. **Bias and Motivation.** Evidence which is sufficiently probative of a witness' possible bias for or against a party warrants its admission into evidence. (United States v. Abel)

2. **Cross-Examination on Nonconviction Misconduct.** A threat to cause physical harm to a person who testifies is sufficiently probative of truthfulness to permit cross-examination of the matter under Fed. R. Evid. 608(b). (United States v. Manske)

3. **Proving Prior Convictions.** In determining whether or not to admit evidence of a prior felony conviction, the trial court has discretion to investigate the underlying facts of the conviction to determine whether or not its admission is more probative than prejudicial. (United States v. Lipscomb)

4. **Proving Prior Convictions.** To raise and preserve for review the claim of improper impeachment with a prior conviction, a defendant must testify at trial. (Luce v. United States)

5. **Prior Inconsistent Statements.** Impeachment by prior inconsistent statement is impermissible if used to get otherwise inadmissible evidence before the jury. (United States v. Webster)

6. **Prior Inconsistent Statements.** Statements obtained in violation of a defendant's Miranda rights may be admitted for impeachment purposes. (Harris v. New York)

7. **Prior Inconsistent Statements.** The use of prearrest silence to impeach a defendant's credibility does not violate the Fifth or Fourteenth Amendments. (Jenkins v. Anderson)

8. **Contradiction.** Suppressed evidence may be used to impeach testimony given by a criminal defendant on cross-examination. (United States v. Havens)

9. **Evidence of Good Character.** Under Rule 608(a) of the Federal Rules of Evidence, character evidence may be used to support a witness, but only after the character of the witness for truthfulness has been attacked by opinion or reputation evidence or otherwise. (United States v. Medical Therapy Sciences)

UNITED STATES v. ABEL
Government (P) v. Convicted bank robber (D)
469 U.S. 45 (1984).

NATURE OF CASE: Appeal from a bank robbery conviction.

FACT SUMMARY: The court of appeals overturned Abel's (D) conviction on the basis that evidence produced to impeach a defense witness was improper in that it suggested the witness was committing perjury due to his membership in a particular organization.

CONCISE RULE OF LAW: Evidence which is sufficiently probative of a witness' possible bias for or against a party warrants its admission into evidence.

FACTS: Abel (D) was arrested and tried for bank robbery. One accomplice who plead guilty prior to trial, Ehle, agreed to testify against Abel (D) at his trial. At trial, Ehle implicated Abel (D), and Abel (D) called a Robert Mills, a cellmate of Ehle in prison. Mills testified that Ehle had admitted to him that he intended to implicate Abel (D) falsely in order to receive more favorable treatment from the government. Ehle was then called back to the stand to testify that he, Mills, and Abel (D) were members of a prison gang which required its members to deny the existence of the organization, and to commit perjury on each others' behalf. This evidence was presented to impeach Mills' prior testimony. Abel (D) objected to the testimony concerning the prison gang on the basis that it was improper impeachment based upon the witness' participation in an organization. Abel (D) was convicted, and appealed. The court of appeals overturned the conviction, and the United States Supreme Court granted review.

ISSUE: Is evidence which is sufficiently probative of a witness' possible bias for or against a party admissible?

HOLDING AND DECISION: (Rehnquist, J.) Yes. Evidence which is sufficiently probative of a witness' possible bias for or against a party warrants its admission into evidence. The fact that Mills belonged to a perjurious organization gives rise to a clear inference that he may be perjuring himself in court. Credibility being the most important aspect of the trier of facts duty, such evidence was clearly relevant and clearly admissible to show bias. The tremendous impact of bias upon a witness' credibility requires that such evidence be admitted. As a result, the trial court properly admitted the evidence, and the conviction must stand. The court of appeals' decision is reversed.

EDITOR'S ANALYSIS: Courts often give wide range in terms of admitting evidence of bias. Because the weight of a witness' testimony is the most important aspect of the trial, any evidence which reasonably could show an inclination towards slanting the facts for or against a particular party is almost always relevant. The objection to such evidence properly falls within the argument

that such evidence is so inflammatory, or so likely to mislead or confuse the jury, that its probative value is outweighed by its prejudicial impact. In this case, the court found that the probative value of the evidence, although somewhat inflammatory, clearly outweighed its prejudicial impact, and therefore admitted the evidence.

QUICKNOTES
IMPEACHMENT - The discrediting of a witness by offering evidence to show that the witness lacks credibility.

NOTES:

UNITED STATES v. MANSKE
Government (P) v. Convicted drug dealer (D)
186 F.3d 770 (7th Cir. 1999).

NATURE OF CASE: Appeal from conviction for conspiracy to distribute cocaine.

FACT SUMMARY: Manske (D) contended that the trial judge erred in granting the government's in limine motion to prevent cross-examination of the government's key witness as to the fact that the witness who was himself a drug dealer had, in prior trials on several occassions, told potential witnesses he would kill them if they testified against him.

CONCISE RULE OF LAW: A threat to cause physical harm to a person who testifies is sufficiently probative of truthfulness to permit cross-examination of the matter under Fed. R. Evid. 608(b).

FACTS: Manske (D) was convicted for conspiracy to distribute cocaine. At trial, the court granted the government's motion in limine to prevent Manske's attorney from cross-examining the prosecution's key witness concerning the fact that the witness, who was himself a drug dealer, had in prior trials, on several occassions, told potential witnesses he would kill them if they testified against him. In support of its motion, the government had successfully argued that threatening to cause physical harm to a person who testifies is not sufficiently probative of truthfulness to permit cross-examination of the matter under Fed. R. Evid. 608(b). Manske (D) appealed, contending that threats calculated to encourage people to break the law are probative of truthfulness under Rule 608(b).

ISSUE: Is threatening to cause physical harm to a person who testifies sufficiently probative of truthfulness to permit cross-examination of the matter under Fed. R. Evid. 608(b)?

HOLDING AND DECISION: (Flaum, J.) Yes. Threatening to cause physical harm to a person who testifies is sufficiently probative of truthfulness to permit cross-examination of the matter under Fed. R. Evid. 608(b). Under Rule 608(b), a witness's specific instances of conduct may only be raised on cross-examination if they are probative of truthfulness or untruthfulness. Here, Pszeniczka, as the government's prime witness, gave highly damaging testimony against Manske (D). The federal district court, however, did not permit Manske (D) to cross-examine Pszeniczka about the latter's statements to potential witnesses in an earlier trial that he would kill them if they testified against him. A witness testified in an earlier trial that Pszeniczka confronted and threatened her for talking to the police, as did other witnesses. Here, the trial judge was incorrect in accepting the government's argument that such statements of Pszeniczka tended only to show a propensity for violence, but was not conduct probative of truthfulness. On the contrary, threats

calculated to encourage people to break the law are probative of truthfulness. These threats supported the defense theory that the government's case rested on an elaborate set-up depending on testimony by Pszeniczka and others who were afraid to contradict him. As a practical matter, it is hard to distinguish between untruthfulness and dishonesty. Reversed and remanded for a new trial.

EDITOR'S ANALYSIS: In rejecting the government's argument in the *Manske* case that the errors were harmless, the court considered the importance of the testimony, the presence or absence of corroborating or contradictory evidence, the extent of cross-examination, and the strength of the government's case. Here, the appellate court reversed the conviction since the errors impacted the cross-examination of three of the government's key witnesses, and assessing one of those witnesses' credibility was "critical" because of the lack of physical evidence.

QUICKNOTES

MOTION IN LIMINE - Motion by one party brought prior to trial to exclude the potential introduction of highly prejudicial evidence.

NOTES:

UNITED STATES v. LIPSCOMB
Government (P) v. Convicted drug dealer (D)
702 F.2d 1049 (D.C. Cir. 1983).

NATURE OF CASE: Appeal from a narcotics conviction.

FACT SUMMARY: Lipscomb (D) contended the trial court erred in allowing the prosecution to impeach him on cross-examination based upon a prior robbery conviction.

CONCISE RULE OF LAW: In determining whether or not to admit evidence of a prior felony conviction, the trial court has discretion to investigate the underlying facts of the conviction to determine whether or not its admission is more probative than prejudicial.

FACTS: Lipscomb (D) was arrested and charged with possession of heroin with intent to distribute. He testified in his own behalf, and was impeached on cross-examination based upon a robbery conviction occurring 8 years prior. Lipscomb (D) objected to the admission of the prior felony conviction on the basis that its prejudicial impact outweighed its probative value. He also argued the court was required to inquire into the underlying facts of that conviction to determine the level of prejudicial value. The court held that a person who would commit an armed robbery would also lie under oath, and therefore it found its impeachment value sufficiently probative to outweigh the prejudicial impact. A second trial was held following Lipscomb's (D) conviction, and he unsuccessfully made a motion in limine to exclude the prior conviction. Due to the failure of this motion, Lipscomb (D) failed to testify and he was convicted. He appealed, contending the trial court erred in admitting the prior felony conviction without undertaking an extensive review of the underlying facts to determine whether or not its probative value outweighed its prejudicial impact.

ISSUE: Does a trial court have discretion to inquire into the facts and circumstances underlying a prior felony conviction to determine whether or not its probative value outweighs its prejudicial impact?

HOLDING AND DECISION: (Wald, J.) Yes. The trial court has discretion to inquire into the underlying facts and circumstances of a prior felony conviction to determine whether or not its probative value outweighs its prejudicial impact on the defendant. Congress in enacting Fed. R. Evid. 609 recognized that the admission of any prior felony conviction has some prejudicial impact upon the defendant. It is the intent of that rule that the trial court exercise discretion in determining the extent of that prejudice. In this regard, the trial court has discretion in determining how deeply it must inquire into the underlying facts and circumstances of the conviction to make this determination. The Government (P) at a minimum must furnish the trial court with the name of the crime in order to establish that it is a felony and the date of conviction to establish that it is less than 10 years old. However, no further information is required under the rule. Unless an abuse of discretion is clearly displayed, the trial court's ruling must stand. As a result, discretion was not abused in this case, and the conviction must be upheld.

EDITOR'S ANALYSIS: The court intentionally issued its opinion on a very broad scale in this case. It specifically declined to establish even general guidelines for determining the extent of the inquiry required of trial courts in this regard. The court felt that this issue is the same as any issue involving the exclusion or admission of evidence, and therefore it must give the trial courts wide discretion in this regard. Any general set of guidelines would necessarily have to be amended as each case presents its unique features.

QUICKNOTES

FED. R. EVID. 609 - Provides that any evidence involving a prior conviction for a crime of dishonesty may not be excluded to impeach a witnesses' credibility.

IMPEACHMENT - The discrediting of a witness by offering evidence to show that the witness lacks credibility.

IN LIMINE - Motion by one party brought prior to trial to exclude the potential introduction of highly prejudicial evidence.

NOTES:

LUCE v. UNITED STATES
Convicted drug dealer (D) v. Government (P)
469 U.S. 38 (1984).

NATURE OF CASE: Appeal from conviction for conspiracy and possession of cocaine with intent to distribute.

FACT SUMMARY: In the Government's (P) action against Luce (D) for conspiracy and possession of cocaine with intent to distribute, Luce (D) contended that the district court's ruling denying Luce's (D) motion to forbid the use of a prior conviction to impeach his credibility was an abuse of discretion.

CONCISE RULE OF LAW: To raise and preserve for review the claim of improper impeachment with a prior conviction, a defendant must testify at trial.

FACTS: Luce (D) was indicted on charges of conspiracy and possession of cocaine with intent to distribute, in violation of 21 U.S.C. §§ 846 and 841(a)(1). During his trial, Luce (D) moved for a ruling to preclude the Government (P) from using a 1974 state conviction to impeach him if he testified. Luce (D) made no commitment that he would testify if the motion was granted and did not make a proffer to the court as to what his testimony would be. In opposing the motion, the Government (P) represented that the conviction was for a serious crime—possession of a controlled substance. The district court ruled that the prior conviction fell within the category of permissible impeachment evidence under Fed. R. Evid. 609(a). Luce (D) did not testify, and the jury returned a guilty verdict. The U.S. Court of Appeals for the 6th Circuit affirmed the district court's decision. The court of appeals refused to consider Luce's (D) contention that the district court abused its discretion in denying Luce's (D) motion in limine without making a specific finding that the probative value of the prior conviction outweighed its prejudicial effect. The court of appeals held that when a defendant does not testify, the court will not review the district court's in limine ruling.

ISSUE: To raise and preserve for review the claim of improper impeachment with a prior conviction, must a defendant testify at trial?

HOLDING AND DECISION: (Burger, C.J.) Yes. To raise and preserve for review the claim of improper impeachment with a prior conviction, a defendant must testify at trial. Under Federal Rule of Evidence 609(a)(1), which directs the court to weigh the probative value of a prior conviction against the prejudicial effect to the defendant, to perform such balancing a court must know the precise nature of the defendant's testimony, which is unknowable when, as here, a defendant does not testify. Were in limine rulings under Rule 609(a) reviewable on appeal, almost any error would result in the windfall of automatic reversal. Requiring Luce (D) to testify in order to preserve Rule 609(a) claims will enable the reviewing court to determine the impact any erroneous impeachment many have had in light of the record as a whole. Affirmed.

EDITOR'S ANALYSIS: As a method of impeachment, evidence of conviction of crime is significant only because it stands as proof of the commission of the underlying criminal act. There is little disagreement from the general proposition that at least some crimes are relevant to credibility. There is, however, much disagreement among cases and commentators about which crimes are usable for this purpose. Traditionally, use of felonies has been accepted and for crimes involving dishonesty or false statement without regard to the grade of the offense.

QUICKNOTES

FED. R. EVID. 609 - Provides that any evidence involving a prior conviction for a crime of dishonesty may not be excluded to impeach a witnesses' credibility.

NOTES:

UNITED STATES v. WEBSTER
Government (P) v. Convicted robber (D)
734 F.2d 1191 (7th Cir. 1984).

NATURE OF CASE: Appeal from conviction of aiding and abetting a bank robbery and receiving stolen funds.

FACT SUMMARY: Webster (D) appealed from his conviction of aiding and abetting a bank robbery and receiving stolen funds, arguing it was impermissible to call a hostile witness for the purpose of introducing inadmissible evidence for impeachment purposes.

CONCISE RULE OF LAW: Impeachment by prior inconsistent statement is impermissible if used to get otherwise inadmissible evidence before the jury.

FACTS: Webster (D) was accused of aiding and abetting a bank robbery and receiving stolen funds. The Government (P) introduced the testimony of King, the bank robber, and then offered prior inconsistent statements by which King inculpated Webster (D). His testimony at trial would have exculpated Webster (D). The Government (P) attempted to introduce King's testimony outside the jury, but defense counsel objected. Webster (D) was convicted and appealed, contending it was impermissible to call a hostile witness for the purpose of introducing inadmissible evidence for impeachment purposes.

ISSUE: Is impeachment by prior inconsistent statement permissible if used to get otherwise inadmissible evidence before the jury?

HOLDING AND DECISION: (Posner, J.) No. Impeachment by prior inconsistent statement is impermissible if used to get otherwise inadmissible evidence before the jury. Using evidence in this way places hearsay evidence as substantive evidence against Webster (D), a result neither contemplated nor authorized by Fed. R. Evid. 607. Here, however, there was no bad faith on the part of the Government (P). The prosecutor did not know what King would say and offered to examine King outside the presence of the jury. The good faith standard strikes the proper balance among competing interests. Affirmed.

EDITOR'S ANALYSIS: Many articles have been written on the delicate subject of impeaching one's own witness. Some argue Webster's (D) position in the present case, that the courts should require surprise and harm before impeachment by prior inconsistent statement is allowed. See 3 A Wigmore, Evidence §§ 896-918 (Chadburn rev. 1970) for background on the issue of impeaching one's own witness.

NOTES:

HARRIS v. NEW YORK
Convicted drug dealer (D) v. Government (P)
401 U.S. 222 (1971).

NATURE OF CASE: Appeal from conviction for selling narcotics.

FACT SUMMARY: Statements obtained in violation of Miranda were admitted in order to impeach Harris' (D) testimony.

CONCISE RULE OF LAW: Statements obtained in violation of a defendant's Miranda rights may be admitted for impeachment purposes.

FACTS: Harris (D) was arrested for selling heroin. He was not given his Miranda rights. While in custody, he admitted that he was selling heroin. At trial Harris (D) took the stand on his own behalf and testified that all he had sold was baking powder in an attempt to defraud the purchaser. He stated that the previously submitted evidence showing that the substance had been heroin had been "cooked up" to frame him. On cross-examination, the prosecution asked him if he had made certain statements during interrogation by the police showing that the bag contained heroin. These statements had not been introduced by the prosecution during its case and are admitted to have been obtained in derogation of Harris' (D) Miranda rights. The prosecution stated that they were being used solely for impeachment. The questions were allowed and Harris (D) was convicted. He claimed that these statements were inadmissible for any purpose.

ISSUE: Are statements obtained in violation of Miranda admissible for impeachment purposes?

HOLDING AND DECISION: (Burger, C.J.) Yes. A defendant cannot perjure himself with impunity because impeachment evidence was obtained in derogation of a constitutionally protected right. The court properly admitted the evidence and gave adequate limiting instructions on the fact that it was only to be considered for impeachment purposes. The conviction is affirmed.

DISSENT: (Brennan, J.) The Constitution denies the state the use of an accused's inadmissible statements on cross-examination to impeach the credibility of an accused's testimony given in his own defense. The Constitution guarantees a defendant the fullest opportunity to meet the accusation against him. An accused must be free to deny all the elements of the case against him without thereby giving leave to the government to introduce by way of rebuttal evidence illegally secured, and therefore not available for its case-in-chief. In this regard, there must be no distinction between statements used on direct as opposed to cross-examination.

EDITOR'S ANALYSIS: As a general rule, no evidence is admissible which resulted from illegal police procedures. It is excluded under the "fruits of the poisonous tree" doctrine. However, the rationale of *Harris* has been extended to other excluded evidence areas for impeachment purposes. The same rationale has been used to support these decisions, i.e., perjury should not be allowed. See *Walder v. U.S.*, 347 U.S. 62 (1954).

NOTES:

JENKINS v. ANDERSON
Convicted felon (D) v. Government (P)
447 U.S. 231 (1980).

NATURE OF CASE: Appeal from a manslaughter conviction.

FACT SUMMARY: Jenkins (D) contended the prosecution's use of his prearrest silence violated his rights under the Fifth and Fourteenth Amendments.

CONCISE RULE OF LAW: The use of prearrest silence to impeach a defendant's credibility does not violate the Fifth or Fourteenth Amendments.

FACTS: Jenkins (D) stabbed and killed Doyle Redding. He was apprehended approximately two weeks later and charged with first-degree murder. On cross-examination the prosecutor elicited testimony that Jenkins (D) failed to go to the police immediately after the stabbing. In closing argument, the prosecutor used this failure to immediately inform the authorities as a form of impeachment of the defendant's credibility. Jenkins (D) was convicted of manslaughter and was sentenced to imprisonment in the state prison. He sought federal habeas corpus relief, which was denied. The United States Supreme Court granted review.

ISSUE: Does the use of prearrest silence to impeach a defendant's credibility violate the Fifth and Fourteenth Amendments?

HOLDING AND DECISION: (Powell, J.) No. The use of prearrest silence to impeach a defendant's credibility does not violate the Fifth or Fourteenth Amendments. Under the Fifth Amendment, a defendant is not required to speak or offer evidence against himself. However, when he voluntarily chooses to give up his right to remain silent, he accepts the consequences of being impeached by his prior prearrest silence. Even though this may discourage the invocation of the right to remain silent, this does not impair to an appreciable extent any of the policies behind the rights involved. As a result, the use of prearrest silence as impeachment does not violate the Fifth Amendment. Further, the Fourteenth Amendment right to fundamental fairness is not violated by this ruling. Even in common law the accused was allowed to be impeached due to a previous failure to state a fact in circumstances under which that fact would have been asserted by an innocent person. As a result, the Fourteenth Amendment is not violated. As a result, the conviction must stand.

EDITOR'S ANALYSIS: In *Raffel v. United States*, 271 U.S. 494 (1926), the Court recognized that the Fifth Amendment is not violated when a defendant who testifies in his own defense is impeached with his prior silence. The basis for this ruling, and upon which the present case is based, is that it is assumed that persons who are innocent will have nothing to hide from the authorities. Thus, if a significant lapse occurs between the commission of the act constituting the criminal offense and the reporting of such act to the authorities, when such is reasonable under the circumstances, that will provide a basis for impeachment. The Court has gone on to indicate that under some circumstances impeachment by silence does violate the Constitution. However, such circumstances involve the advice of the right to remain silent, and the exercise of such right. The difference in this case, as pointed out by the Court, was that the defendant was under no legal arrest, and therefore was not exercising a right to remain silent. As a result, the use of such silence could be the basis for impeachment.

QUICKNOTES

HABEAS CORPUS - A proceeding in which a defendant brings a writ to compel a judicial determination of whether he is lawfully being held in custody.

IMPEACHMENT - The discrediting of a witness by offering evidence to show that the witness lacks credibility.

NOTES:

UNITED STATES v. HAVENS
Government (P) v. Convicted drug dealer (D)
446 U.S. 620 (1980).

NATURE OF CASE: Appeal of drug-related conviction.

FACT SUMMARY: The Government (P) used suppressed evidence to impeach testimony given by Havens (D) on cross-examination.

CONCISE RULE OF LAW: Suppressed evidence may be used to impeach testimony given by a criminal defendant on cross-examination.

FACTS: Havens (D) was arrested when companion McLeroth was found by Customs to have cocaine hidden in pockets sewn onto an undershirt he wore. A T-shirt with cutout patterns matching the pockets sewn onto McLeroth's shirt was found in Havens' (D) suitcase. At trial, the court suppressed the T-shirt. Havens (D), testifying in his defense, denied knowledge of the T-shirt during cross-examination. In rebuttal, the Government (P) introduced the shirt over Havens' (D) objection. Havens (D) was convicted, but the court of appeals reversed, holding that suppressed evidence could be admitted only in rebuttal to contradict testimony given on direct. The Supreme Court granted certiorari.

ISSUE: May suppressed evidence be used to impeach testimony given by a criminal defendant on cross-examination?

HOLDING AND DECISION: (White, J.) Yes. Suppressed evidence may be used to impeach testimony given by a criminal defendant on cross-examination. This Court has already held that such evidence may be introduced to rebut testimony given on direct. The Court ruled that the purpose of the exclusionary rule is fully served by denying the Government (P) the use of illegally obtained evidence in its case-in-chief. If a defendant chooses to testify and lies, the Government (P) should be able to rebut the testimony with any available means; the truthfinding function of the trial process demands it. There is no reason not to apply this to cross-examination testimony, as a defendant is under the same obligation to tell the truth on cross. The evidence here was, therefore, properly admitted. Reversed.

DISSENT: (Brennan, J.) A prosecutor should not be allowed to use cross-examination as a vehicle to gain admission to otherwise inadmissible evidence.

EDITOR'S ANALYSIS: The Court has never come close to doing away with the exclusionary rule, but since the late 1960s has availed itself of numerous opportunities to limit it. The present case is an illustration of this. Another such case was *Harris v. New York*, 401 U.S. 222 (1971), which permits inadmissible statements to be used for impeachment.

UNITED STATES v. MEDICAL THERAPY SCIENCES
Government (P) v. Health care company (D)
583 F.2d 36 (2d Cir. 1978).

NATURE OF CASE: Appeal from criminal convictions.

FACT SUMMARY: The United States (P) brought out on direct examination the fact that one of its witnesses had suffered prior criminal convictions, and it then offered character evidence to bolster her credibility.

CONCISE RULE OF LAW: Under Rule 608(a) of the Federal Rules of Evidence, character evidence may be used to support a witness, but only after the character of the witness for truthfulness has been attacked by opinion or reputation evidence or otherwise.

FACTS: In support of its charges that Berman (D) and his company, Medical Therapy Sciences (D), had filed false claims to obtain Medicare payments, the United States (P) offered testimony by Barbara Russell, formerly a trusted employee and personal intimate of Berman (D). On direct, the Government (P) brought out the fact that she had prior criminal convictions so that the jury would not think it was attempting to hide such information if, as expected, it came out on cross-examination. Cross-examination of Russell included sharp questioning about her prior convictions, which were predicated on activities characterized as fraudulent. In appealing the resulting conviction, Berman (D) and Medical Therapy Sciences (D) argued that the Government (P) should not have been permitted to present character evidence in its rebuttal case to support Russell's credibility inasmuch as it was the Government (P) who had brought up the prior convictions and not the defense who had placed her character at issue.

ISSUE: Is character evidence in support of a witness admissible only after the character of the witness for truthfulness has been attacked?

HOLDING AND DECISION: (Moore, J.) Yes. Rule 608(a) of the Federal Rules of Evidence provides that character evidence may be used to support a witness, but limits its use so that "evidence of truthful character is admissible only after the character of the witness for truthfulness has been attacked by opinion or reputation evidence or otherwise." It contains no limitation that precludes a party from offering character evidence under circumstances where it anticipates impeachment, so the fact that the Government (P) here was the first to bring up the issue of Russell's credibility does not preclude it from thereafter offering character evidence in support of her. Under the particular circumstances of this case, the trial court did not abuse its discretion in permitting such evidence. Affirmed.

EDITOR'S ANALYSIS: A rule allowing evidence in support of a witness' character to be offered only if the other party first put character in issue would be unfair. It would force the prosecutor to conceal the bad record of his witness from the jury to retain his right to submit character evidence should the issue arise. That hardly seems conducive to a fair and just trial by jury.

_____

QUICKNOTES

DIRECT EXAMINATION - The initial interrogation of a witness, conducted by the party who called the witness.

NOTES:

CHAPTER 9
OPINION AND EXPERT TESTIMONY;
SCIENTIFIC EVIDENCE

QUICK REFERENCE RULES OF LAW

1. **Defining a Standard.** If scientific knowledge will assist the trier of fact to understand the evidence or to determine a fact in issue, a witness qualified as an expert by knowledge, skill, experience, training, or education may testify thereto in the form of an opinion or otherwise. (Daubert v. Merrell Dow Phamaceuticals)

2. **Defining a Standard.** A trial court must examine the reliability of expert testimony for not only "scientific" knowledge but "technical" or over "specialized" knowledge as well, and may flexibly apply one or more of Daubert's specific factors to determine the admissibility of a technical expert's testimony based on its relevancy and reliability. (Kumho Tire Company, Ltd. v. Carmichael)

3. **DNA Evidence.** DNA evidence is admissible and satisfies the Daubert standard in that it is of assistance to the trier of fact, possesses a reasonable amount of certainty, and is widely relied upon by experts in the field of forensics. (State v. Moore)

DAUBERT v. MERRELL DOW PHARMACEUTICALS

Drug-related injured person (P) v. Pharmaceutical company (D)

509 U.S. 579 (1993).

NATURE OF CASE: Appeal from a grant of defendant's motion for summary judgment in an action to recover damages for personal injuries.

FACT SUMMARY: In Daubert's (P) suit to recover damages for serious birth defects allegedly caused by a drug marketed by Merrell Dow (D), the court granted Merrell Dow's (D) motion for summary judgment after applying the general acceptance, or "Frye," rule to the scientific evidence of Daubert's (P) expert witnesses.

CONCISE RULE OF LAW: If scientific knowledge will assist the trier of fact to understand the evidence or to determine a fact in issue, a witness qualified as an expert by knowledge, skill, experience, training, or education may testify thereto in the form of an opinion or otherwise.

FACTS: Jason Daubert (P) and Eric Schuller (P) brought this suit for damages, alleging that their serious birth defects had been caused by their mothers' ingestion of Bendectin, a drug marketed by Merrell Dow (D). Merrell Dow (D) moved for summary judgment, submitting an affidavit by its expert witness, who concluded, after reviewing more than thirty published studies, that maternal use of Bendectin during the first trimester of pregnancy was not a risk factor for human birth defects. Daubert's (P) and Schuller's (P) eight experts conducted their own studies and reanalyzed previously published studies, concluding that Bendectin can cause birth defects. The court granted Merrell Dow's (D) motion for summary judgment, holding that scientific evidence must be generally accepted to be admissible. The court of appeals affirmed. Daubert (P) and Schuller (P) appealed.

ISSUE: If scientific knowledge will assist the trier of fact to understand the evidence or to determine a fact in issue, may a witness qualified as an expert by knowledge, skill, experience, training, or education testify thereto in the form of an opinion or otherwise?

HOLDING AND DECISION: (Blackmun, J.) Yes. If scientific knowledge will assist the trier of fact to understand the evidence or to determine a fact in issue, a witness qualified as an expert by knowledge, skill, experience, training, or education may testify thereto in the form of an opinion or otherwise. The general acceptance test established by *Frye v. United States*, 293 F. 1013 (D.C. Cir.1923), has been displaced by the Federal Rules of Evidence. The current inquiry to be made under Fed. R. Evid. 702 is the scientific validity, and thus the evidentiary relevance and reliability, of the principles underlying a proposed submission. Unlike an ordinary witness, an expert is permitted wide latitude to offer opinions. Accordingly, the judgment of the court of appeals is vacated, and the case is remanded for further proceedings.

CONCURRENCE AND DISSENT: (Rehnquist, C.J.) The Court correctly concluded that the enactment of the Fed. R. Evid. replaced the "general acceptance" doctrine of *Frye v. United States*, 293 F. 1013 (D.C. Cir. 1923). The Court went too far, however, in concocting a new test based only on general principles and observations, and not upon the facts of the case at hand. The standards the majority set out as a substitute for the Frye "general acceptance" test are not all that different from it, except that they are even more vague. While judges do need to make some determinations as to the relevance and validity of scientific expert testimony, it is beyond their experience and resources to expect them to go through the analysis the majority describes. It is certain that lower federal courts will have a very difficult time interpreting not only the scientific evidence they are faced with, but also the majority opinion.

EDITOR'S ANALYSIS: The Rules of Evidence assign to the trial judge the task of ensuring that an expert's testimony both rests on a reliable foundation and is relevant to the task at hand. Pertinent evidence based on scientifically valid principles will satisfy those demands. While publication, peer review, and general acceptance can have a bearing on the court's inquiry, they are not dispositive.

NOTES:

KUMHO TIRE CO., LTD. v. CARMICHAEL

Tire manufacturer and distributor (D) v. Accident victim (P)

526 U.S. 137 (1998).

NATURE OF CASE: Review of order declaring evidence inadmissible and judgment for defendant.

FACT SUMMARY: Carmichael (P) claimed that his expert witness testimony was improperly excluded at trial and successfully appealed the trial court's application of the *Daubert* factors to determine the admissibility of technical evidence.

CONCISE RULE OF LAW: A trial court must examine the reliability of expert testimony for not only "scientific" knowledge but "technical" or over "specialized" knowledge as well, and may flexibly apply one or more of *Daubert*'s specific factors to determine the admissibility of a technical expert's testimony based on its relevancy and reliability.

FACTS: The right rear tire on Carmichael's (P) minivan blew out and caused an accident in which one passenger died and others were severely injured. Carmichael (P) alleged that the tire was defective and sued the manufacturer, Kumho (D). Carmichael (P) rested his case in significant part upon deposition testimony provided by an expert in tire failure analysis, who intended to testify in support of his conclusion. Kumho's (D) motion to exclude that testimony was granted, on the ground that the tire expert's methodology failed Rule 702's reliability requirement. The specific factors discussed in *Daubert v. Merrill Dow Pharmaceuticals, Inc.*, 509 U.S. 579 (1993) to determine whether scientific expert testimony is both relevant and reliable were applied by the court. These factors include testing, peer review, error rules, and the "acceptability" in the relevant scientific community. The court agreed with Kumho (D) that it should act as a *Daubert*-type gatekeeper, even though one might consider the testimony technical, rather than scientific. Carmichael's (P) motion for reconsideration was then granted, but the court later affirmed its earlier order and granted Kumho's (D) motion for summary judgment. The Eleventh Circuit reversed, concluding that the testimony fell outside the scope of *Daubert*, whose holding was expressly limited to the application of scientific principles, and not to skill or experience-based observation. Kumho (D) appealed, and the Supreme Court granted certiorari.

ISSUE: Must a trial court examine the reliability of expert testimony (for not only "scientific" knowledge, but "technical" or other "specialized" knowledge as well and could the court flexibly apply one or more of *Daubert's* specific factors to determine the admissibility of a technical expert's testimony based on its relevancy and reliability?

HOLDING AND DECISION: (Breyer, J.) Yes. A trial court must examine the reliability of expert testimony for not only "scientific"

knowledge but "technical" or over "specialized" knowledge as well, and may flexibly apply one or more of *Daubert's* specific factors to determine the admissibility of a technical expert's testimony based on its relevancy and reliability. A trial judge has a special obligation to ensure that any and all scientific testimony is not only relevant, but reliable. *Daubert* applies to technical or other specialized, non-specific knowledge where expert testimony is being proffered. Thus, some of *Daubert's* questions can help to evaluate the reliability even of experience-based testimony. Whether *Daubert's* specific factors are, or are not, reasonable measures of reliability in a particular case is a matter that the law grants the trial judge broad latitude to determine. The trial judge in this case determined that the testimony fell outside the area where experts might reasonably differ, and where the jury must decide among the conflicting views of different experts, even though the evidence is shaky. The doubts that triggered the trial court's initial inquiry here were reasonable, as was the court's ultimate conclusion. Rule 702 grants the district judge the discretionary authority, reviewable for its abuse, to determine reliability in light of the particular facts and circumstances of the particular case. The district court did not abuse its discretionary authority in his case. Reversed.

CONCURRENCE: (Scalia, J.) Trial judges have discretion to "choose among *reasonable* means" of appraising science. They do not have discretion to perform the gatekeeping responsibility "inadequately."

CONCURRENCE AND DISSENT: (Stevens, J.) The question whether Carlson should have been allowed to testify should be decided by the trial court under the correct standard as set forth in this opinion.

EDITOR'S ANALYSIS: Justice Stevens concurred with the first two parts of the court's decision here, but dissented from the disposition of the case. He wrote that the question of the exclusion of the expert testimony should be decided by the court of appeals since it involved a study of the record. *Daubert* itself made clear that its list of factors was meant to be helpful, not definitive.

QUICKNOTES

EXPERT TESTIMONY - Testimonial evidence about a complex area of subject matter relevant to trial, presented by a person competent to inform the trier of fact due to specialized knowledge or training.

EXPERT WITNESS - A witness providing testimony at trial who is specially qualified regarding the particular subject matter involved.

STATE v. MOORE
Government (P) v. Indicted murderer (D)
Sup. Ct. of Mont., 885 P.2d 457 (1994)

NATURE OF CASE: Appeal by defendant on ruling on admissibility of DNA evidence.

FACT SUMMARY: Moore (D) was charged with the murder of Brisbin, whose body was never found, although DNA analysis of blood and muscle tissue found in Moore's car were linked to the victim.

CONCISE RULE OF LAW: DNA evidence is admissible and satisfies the Daubert standard in that it is of assistance to the trier of fact, possesses a reasonable amount of certainty, and is widely relied upon by experts in the field of forensics.

FACTS: Brad Brisbin disappeared without a trace on the morning of November 9, 1990. His body was never recovered, but his wife testified that he was on his way to meet Moore (D) at a truckstop. There was proof that Moore's (D) truck was seen near the location later that same morning. When questioned about Brisbin, Moore (D) gave several conflicting responses as to when and where he had last seen the victim. Small pieces of human brain and muscle tissue were discovered in the cab of Moore's (D) truck. DNA studies were conducted on them at two different laboratories using RFLP analysis. The findings linked the samples tested to the biological father of the victim's children and to the victim's mother. At trial, the defense filed a motion to exclude this evidence, which was overruled. The defense filed a second motion to exclude testimony describing statistical analysis and correlations that the DNA evidence presented could be linked to the defendant's children. This motion was granted.

ISSUE: Is DNA evidence admissible as expert scientific testimony following the standard set out in Daubert?

HOLDING AND DECISION: Yes. DNA evidence obtained using RFLP analysis satisfies the standards set out by the Supreme Court in *Daubert v. Merrell Dow Pharmaceuticals*, 509 U.S. 579 (1993). Although there may be slight inconsistencies in test results, these do not require exclusion of the evidence. DNA evidence is of great value for forensic purposes because no two individuals have the identical DNA, with the exception of identical twins. In addition, because the defense previously filed a motion to exclude statistical analysis on the probability of a match of the DNA evidence, they are prevented from claiming at this time that keeping out this data would be misleading. Affirmed.

EDITOR'S ANALYSIS: The holding in Moore is significant because it sets a precedent for the acceptance of certain types of DNA evidence. Although the case is from Montana, it will likely be cited in other states and given heavy consideration. It will also be an important reference as DNA technologies progress and new types of genetic mapping are developed.

NOTES:

10

CHAPTER 10
BURDENS OF PROOF AND PRESUMPTIONS

QUICK REFERENCE RULES OF LAW

1. **Burdens and Presumptions in Civil Cases.** Once a prima facie case of employment discrimination has been established, the burden shifts to the employer-defendant to articulate some legitimate, nondiscriminatory reason for the employee's rejection—and that is all that is required at that point. (Texas Department of Community Affairs v. Burdine)

2. **Burden of Persuasion.** Requiring a murder defendant to prove the affirmative defense of extreme emotional disturbance is not a violation of his constitutional rights under the Fourteenth Amendment Due Process Clause. (Patterson v. New York)

3. **Presumptions and Inferences.** Due process prohibits instructing the jury, in a case in which intent is an element of the crime charged, that "the law presumes that a person intended the ordinary consequences of his voluntary acts." (Sandstrom v. Montana)

4. **Presumptions and Inferences.** For a permissible presumption to be constitutional, there must be a rational connection between the basic facts that the prosecution proved and the ultimate fact presumed, and the ultimate fact presumed must be more likely than not to flow from the facts proved. (County of Ulster v. Allen)

TEXAS DEPARTMENT OF COMMUNITY AFFAIRS v. BURDINE

Government agency (D) v. Employee (P)
450 U.S. 248 (1981).

NATURE OF CASE: Employment discrimination suit.

FACT SUMMARY: Once Burdine (P) established a prima facie case of gender based discrimination, the question became the nature of the burden that thereby shifted to her employer, the Department (D).

CONCISE RULE OF LAW: Once a prima facie case of employment discrimination has been established, the burden shifts to the employer-defendant to articulate some legitimate, nondiscriminatory reason for the employee's rejection—and that is all that is required at that point.

FACTS: Burdine (P) brought an employment discrimination suit against the Department (D) under Title VII of the Civil Rights Act, alleging gender-based discrimination. The trial court held that none of the decisions made by the Department (D) had been based on gender discrimination. The court of appeals reversed the trial court's finding that the Department (D) had rebutted Burdine's (P) prima facie case of gender discrimination. It reiterated its view that the defendant in a Title VII case must rebut a prima facie case of discrimination by proving by a preponderance of the evidence the existence of legitimate nondiscriminatory reasons for the employment action and that those hired or promoted were better qualified than the plaintiff-employee.

ISSUE: Is the only burden an employer must meet to rebut a prima facie case of employment discrimination that of articulating some legitimate, nondiscriminatory reason for its action?

HOLDING AND DECISION: (Powell, J.) Yes. When the plaintiff in a Title VII case alleging discriminatory treatment establishes a prima facie case of discrimination by a preponderance of the evidence, this effectively creates a presumption that the employer unlawfully discriminated. The burden then shifts to the employer-defendant to rebut the presumption of discrimination by articulating some legitimate, nondiscriminatory reason for the employment action it took. The employer is not required to assume the greater burden that the court of appeals would place on him. Once the employer-defendant articulates a legitimate, nondiscriminatory reason for its action, the plaintiff-employee then has the opportunity to prove by a preponderance of the evidence that the legitimate reasons offered by the employer-defendant were not its true reasons, but were a pretext for discrimination. Since the court of appeals erred in its pronouncement of the burden faced by the Department (D), its judgment must be vacated and the case remanded.

EDITOR'S ANALYSIS: The Court's use of the word "presumption" is unique. In cases involving sex or race discrimination claims, the courts usually couch their decisions in terms of shifting "burdens" without employing that term. In fact, none of the statutes that underlie such cases uses the term either.

QUICKNOTES

BURDEN OF PROOF - The duty of a party to introduce evidence to support a fact that is in dispute in an action.

PRIMA FACIE CASE - An action where the plaintiff introduces sufficient evidence to submit the issue to the judge or jury for determination.

NOTES:

PATTERSON v. NEW YORK
Murderer (D) v. Government (P)
432 U.S. 197 (1977)

NATURE OF CASE: Appeal from a murder conviction.

FACT SUMMARY: Gordon Patterson (D), convicted of the murder of his estranged wife's boyfriend, appealed on the grounds that the jury instructions which placed on Patterson (D) the burden of proving that he acted under extreme emotional distress were a violation of his Fourteenth Amendment Due Process rights.

CONCISE RULE OF LAW: Requiring a murder defendant to prove the affirmative defense of extreme emotional disturbance is not a violation of his constitutional rights under the Fourteenth Amendment Due Process Clause.

FACTS: Gordon Patterson (D) and his wife Roberta separated after a brief and unstable marriage. Following the breakup, Roberta resumed a relationship with John Northrup, a neighbor and the man to whom she had been engaged prior to her marriage to Patterson (D). One evening, Patterson (D) borrowed a rifle and went to the residence of Roberta's father. After observing Roberta and Northrup in a state of semiundress from a window outside the home, Patterson (D) entered the residence and shot Northrup twice in the head, killing him. Patterson (D) confessed before trial to killing Northrup, but at trial raised the defense of extreme emotional disturbance. On appeal, Patterson (D) argued that instructions given to the jury violated his constitutional rights under the Fourteenth Amendment Due Process Clause because they required him to prove an element of the charged offense. The New York Court of Appeals affirmed the conviction holding that the burden of proving the elements of the crime had not shifted to Patterson (D). The court stated that the elements of the defense of extreme emotional distress are distinct from those of the charged offense of murder, and therefore no violation of rights occurred. The Supreme Court granted review.

ISSUE: Is requiring a murder defendant to prove the affirmative defense of extreme emotional disturbance a violation of his constitutional rights under the Fourteenth Amendment Due Process Clause?

HOLDING AND DECISION: (White, J.) No. Because the burden of proof placed upon Patterson (D) in proving the defense of extreme emotional distress did not require him to negate any element of the charged crime of murder, there was no violation of his constitutional rights. The State (P) successfully carried its burden of proving every element required in the New York murder statute. The affirmative defense is a totally separate issue on which it is acceptable to require the defendant to bear the burden of persuasion. Just because mitigating evidence of a crime may be considered, it does not mean that the State has the burden of proving its nonexistence. This case is differentiated from *Mullaney v. Wilbur*, 421 U.S. 684 (1975), in which a Maine statute was found to be unconstitutional because that statute provided for a presumption of an element of the offense which the defendant could then rebut. Affirmed.

DISSENT: (Powell, J.) The majority opinion is contrary to the basic rationale of the holding in Mullaney and is a violation of Patterson's (D) rights under the Mullaney standard. In addition, the majority opinion allows legislatures too broad of a discretion in the drafting of criminal statutes. This will likely result in the shifting of burdens of proof from the prosecution to the defense according to the whims of the legislature, thereby sidestepping important constitutional safeguards.

EDITOR'S ANALYSIS: The issues raised by the dissent regarding legislative discretion are of significant concern. Following the rationale of the majority in Patterson, a murder statute could be written without an element of intent, requiring only that the prosecution show that an individual caused the death of another, and that the defendant prove all mitigating evidence. Another possible result if Patterson is taken to extremes could be that mitigating evidence would only be permitted during sentencing.

QUICKNOTES

FOURTEENTH AMENDMENT DUE PROCESS CLAUSE - Provides that protections mandated by the constitution and observed by the federal government are equally applicable, and therefor must be observed by the States.

NOTES:

SANDSTROM v. MONTANA
Murderer (D) v. Government (P)
442 U.S. 510 (1979).

NATURE OF CASE: Appeal from a conviction of "deliberate homicide."

FACT SUMMARY: At Sandstrom's (D) trial for deliberate homicide, of which "intent" is an element, the jury was instructed that the law presumed a person intends the ordinary consequences of his acts.

CONCISE RULE OF LAW: Due process prohibits instructing the jury, in a case in which intent is an element of the crime charged, that "the law presumes that a person intended the ordinary consequences of his voluntary acts."

FACTS: After a jury instruction that "the law presumes that a person intends the ordinary consequences of his voluntary acts," Sandstrom (D) was convicted of "deliberate homicide" for "purposely or knowingly causing the death of Annie Jessen." His defense had been that a personality disorder aggravated by alcohol consumption prevented his acting "purposely" or "knowingly." The Montana Supreme Court, hearing Sandstrom's (D) appeal, agreed with his contention that Mullaney v. Wilbur, in re Winship, and Patterson v. New York held that due process prohibited a state from shifting to a defendant the burden of disproving an element of the crime charged. However, it viewed the instruction at issue as having merely placed on Sandstrom (D) the burden of producing some evidence that he did not intend the ordinary consequences of his acts and not as having required him to disprove that he acted "purposely" or "knowingly." Thus, it upheld the conviction.

ISSUE: Does it violate due process to charge the jury, in a case in which intent is an element of the crime charged, that "the law presumes a person intended the ordinary consequences of his acts?"

HOLDING AND DECISION: (Brennan, J.) Yes. Due process requires that a state prove every element of a criminal offense beyond a reasonable doubt, and this prohibits instructing the jury, in a case in which intent is an element of the crime charged, that "the law presumes that a person intended the ordinary consequences of his voluntary acts." In this case, a reasonable juror could have given the presumption at issue conclusive of persuasion-shifting effect, and that would violate the Due Process Clause by alleviating the state's burden of proving one element of the crime charged. Reversed and remanded.

EDITOR'S ANALYSIS: In 1 Jones, The Law of Evidence, §§ 9-10, pp. 16-20 (5th ed. 1958), the author sees use of the word "presumption" as indicating a particular conclusion must be drawn on the basis of particular proved facts unless and until it is rebutted by some evidence. Use of the word "inference," however, permits the jury to choose whether or not to draw the conclusion.

QUICKNOTES

PRESUMPTION - A rule of law requiring the court to presume certain facts to be true based on the existence of other facts, thereby shifting the burden of proof to the party against whom the presumption is asserted to rebut.

NOTES:

COUNTY OF ULSTER v. ALLEN
Government (P) v. Convict (D)
442 U.S. 140 (1979).

NATURE OF CASE: Appeal from affirmance of issuance of habeas corpus.

FACT SUMMARY: Allen (D) claimed his criminal conviction was obtained by use of an unconstitutional statutory presumption making the presence of a firearm in an automobile presumptive evidence of its illegal possession by all persons then occupying the vehicle.

CONCISE RULE OF LAW: For a permissible presumption to be constitutional, there must be a rational connection between the basic facts that the prosecution proved and the ultimate fact presumed, and the ultimate fact presumed must be more likely than not to flow from the facts proved.

FACTS: New York law made the presence of a firearm in an automobile presumptive evidence of its illegal possession by all persons then occupying the vehicle. Allen (D) and others suffered a criminal conviction in a trial in which this statutory presumption was applied under instructions which were vague but which arguably suggested it was permissible rather than mandatory. After a writ of habeas corpus was granted on the ground that the statute was unconstitutional and an appellate affirmance of that decision, the United States Supreme Court addressed the question.

ISSUE: Does the constitutionality of a permissible presumption depend on there being a rational connection between the basic facts which the prosecution proved and the ultimate fact presumed and on the latter being more likely than not to flow from the former?

HOLDING AND DECISION: (Stevens, J.) Yes. For a permissible presumption to be constitutional, there must be a rational connection between the basic facts which the prosecution proved and the ultimate fact presumed and that the latter is more likely than not to flow from the former. The circumstances of this case indicate the presumption at issue was treated as being permissive, so the argument that a reasonable doubt standard should be used to assess its constitutional validity simply will not stand. Under the appropriate standard for permissive presumptions, the presumption here was constitutional. Reversed.

DISSENT: (Powell, J.) This presumption violates due process because it does not fairly reflect what common sense and experience tell us about passengers in automobiles and the possession of handguns.

EDITOR'S ANALYSIS: The Supreme Court has held that the existence of other evidence in the record sufficient to support a conviction is relevant in analyzing a purely permissive presumption but not in analyzing a mandatory presumption. *Turner v. United States*, 319 U.S. 463 (1970); *Leary v. United States*, 395 U.S. 6 (1969); *United States v. Romano*, 382 U.S. 136 (1965).

QUICKNOTES

PRESUMPTION - A rule of law requiring the court to presume certain facts to be true based on the existence of other facts, thereby shifting the burden of proof to the party against whom the presumption is asserted to rebut.

NOTES:

11

CHAPTER 11
JUDICIAL NOTICE

QUICK REFERENCE RULES OF LAW

1. **Judicial Notice of Adjudicative Facts.** A court may not take judicial notice of a fact merely because the judge has knowledge of that fact in his personal capacity. (Government of the Virgin Islands v. Gereau)

2. **Judicial Notice in Criminal Cases.** Failure to plead a fact in a criminal proceeding may not be cured by judicial notice. (United States v. Jones)

3. **Judicial Notice of Legislative Facts.** A court may take judicial notice of legislative findings as matters of general knowledge. (Muller v. Oregon)

4. **Judicial Notice of Legislative Facts.** Courts may take judicial notice of scientific studies when analyzing a statute. (Houser v. State)

5. **The Problem of Classification.** Under the Federal Rules of Evidence, a court is not precluded from instructing the jury that it must accept as conclusive a "legislative" fact of which the court has taken judicial notice, i.e., a fact, truth, or pronouncement that does not change from case to case but applies universally. (United States v. Gould)

GOVERNMENT OF THE VIRGIN ISLANDS v. GEREAU
Government (P) v. Convicted felon (D)
523 F.2d 140 (3d Cir. 1975).

NATURE OF CASE: Appeal of multiple felony conviction.

FACT SUMMARY: A court took judicial notice of a fact personally known to the sitting judge.

CONCISE RULE OF LAW: A court may not take judicial notice of a fact merely because the judge has knowledge of that fact in his personal capacity.

FACTS: Gereau (D), after a nine-day jury deliberation, was convicted of murder, assault, and robbery. Gereau (D) sought a new trial based on the statements of one juror who testified that another had merely joined in the verdict to be able to go home. That juror denied the statements. The court, taking judicial notice of the fact, known to the trial judge, that the juror in question liked jury duty, denied the motion. Gereau (D) appealed.

ISSUE: May a court take judicial notice of a fact merely because the judge has knowledge of that fact in his personal capacity?

HOLDING AND DECISION: (Per curiam) No. A court may not take judicial notice of a fact merely because the judge has knowledge of that fact in his personal capacity. Facts of which judicial notice may be taken are those beyond a reasonable controversy, either as matters of common knowledge or capable of immediate determination by recourse to indisputably accurate sources. When a fact does not fall within this definition, judicial notice of it may not be taken, even if the judge personally knows it to be true. Here, the motives of the juror were not of the type of fact amenable to judicial notice, and the court's actions were improper. [The court went on to hold the error harmless and affirmed.]

EDITOR'S ANALYSIS: While the Federal Rules of Evidence tend to be broad in terms of admissible evidence, judicial notice is an exception. Fed. R. Evid. 201(b), which covers judicial notice of adjudicative facts, creates an exacting standard. Any fact not plainly self-evident will have a hard time being admitted under the rule.

QUICKNOTES
JUDICIAL NOTICE - The discretion of a court to recognize certain well-known facts as being true, without the necessity of a party introducing evidence to establish the truth of the fact.

NOTES:

UNITED STATES v. JONES
Government (P) v. Wire tapper (D)
580 F.2d 219 (1978).

NATURE OF CASE: Appeal from acquittal of illegal interception of telephone calls.

FACT SUMMARY: Jones (D) was acquitted of intercepting telephone calls illegally because the Government (P) failed to allege that the maker of the telephone, South Central Bell, was a common carrier providing facilities for interstate communication.

CONCISE RULE OF LAW: Failure to plead a fact in a criminal proceeding may not be cured by judicial notice.

FACTS: Jones (D) was charged with illegally intercepting telephone conversations by tapping the telephone of his estranged wife. The telephone was made by South Central Bell, part of an international corporation providing communications services throughout the world. The statute under which Jones (D) was charged required that the interception be from equipment of a common carrier providing facilities for the transmission of interstate communications. The Government (P) failed to allege South Central Bell's status as such a carrier and Jones (D) was accordingly acquitted despite a guilty verdict. The Government (P) appealed, seeking to cure the pleading defect by requesting judicial notice of Bell's status.

ISSUE: May a failure to plead a fact in a criminal proceeding be cured by judicial notice?

HOLDING AND DECISION: (Engel, J.) No. While the Fed. R. Evid. 201(f) permits the request of judicial notice at any state of a proceeding, even on appeal, the value of judicial notice is different in a criminal proceeding such as this one than in a civil action. In a civil action, the jury must regard judicially noticed facts as conclusively established. However, in a criminal proceeding, the jury must pass on facts that are judicially noticed, despite the notice. Thus, even if judicial notice is taken in this case of South Central Bell's status as an interstate carrier, the jury would not be required to accept the fact. Thus, failure to plead a fact in a criminal proceeding may not be cured by judicial notice. The jury's right to reject the judicially noticed fact cannot be taken away by granting notice after the jury is discharged.

EDITOR'S ANALYSIS: The neglect of the Government's (P) attorney is on the one hand exactly the kind of mistake that Fed. R. Evid. 201(f) is intended to cure by allowing judicial notice on appeal. However, the right of the defendant to have the jury render its verdict with the ability to reject the judicially noticed fact outweighs the policy for correction on appeal. The peculiar result in this case has been criticized.

QUICKNOTES

JUDICIAL NOTICE - The discretion of a court to recognize certain well-known facts as being true, without the necessity of a party introducing evidence to establish the truth of the fact.

NOTES:

MULLER v. OREGON
Statutue challenger (P) v. State (D)
208 U.S. 412 (1907).

NATURE OF CASE: Action challenging the constitutionality of a state labor statute.

FACT SUMMARY: In a challenge to a state labor law, the Supreme Court took judicial notice of certain legislative findings.

CONCISE RULE OF LAW: A court may take judicial notice of legislative findings as matters of general knowledge.

FACTS: A challenge was made to an Oregon (D) statute setting a maximum work day for women. In reviewing a lower court holding finding the statute constitutional, the Supreme Court had to consider whether to take judicial notice of certain facts found by the Oregon state legislature.

ISSUE: May a court take judicial notice of legislative findings as matters of general knowledge?

HOLDING AND DECISION: (Brewer, J.) Yes. A court may take judicial notice of legislative findings as matters of general knowledge. A court may take judicial notice of all matters of general knowledge. A legislative finding is significant as to whether a particular fact is of common knowledge, and therefore judicial notice may be taken of these facts. [The Court went on to uphold the statute.]

EDITOR'S ANALYSIS: The sort of facts that may be contained in legislative findings is broad indeed. Legislatures often pore over voluminous reports before legislation is enacted. In this action, for instance, over 90 committee reports were utilized.

QUICKNOTES
JUDICIAL NOTICE - The discretion of a court to recognize certain well-known facts as being true, without the necessity of a party introducing evidence to establish the truth of the fact.

HOUSER v. STATE
Challenger of statute (P) v. State (D)
Wash. Sup. Ct., 540 P. 2d 412 (1975).

NATURE OF CASE: Review of dismissal of action challenging state liquor regulations.

FACT SUMMARY: In considering the rationality of a statute, a court took judicial notice of scientific studies.

CONCISE RULE OF LAW: Courts may take judicial notice of scientific studies when analyzing a statute.

FACTS: Houser (P) challenged Washington's minimum age law on alcohol consumption, alleging equal protection violations. In concluding that the law was rationally related to a legitimate governmental purpose, the trial court took judicial notice of certain scientific studies. The trial court granted summary judgment in favor of the State (D). The appellate court affirmed. The state supreme court granted review.

ISSUE: May courts take judicial notice of scientific studies when analyzing a statute?

HOLDING AND DECISION: (Utter, J.) Yes. Courts may take judicial notice of scientific studies when analyzing a statute. While a court should not judicially notice a controverted scientific treatise or study when resolving a factual dispute, a court may ascertain as it sees fit any fact that is merely a ground for laying down a rule of law. Here, the court had only to conclude that the statute in question was rational. Evidence of its rationality was the fact that scientific studies existed validating the legislative decision. The trial court correctly noticed their existence. It did not and did not need to validate their accuracy. Affirmed.

EDITOR'S ANALYSIS: In this case, the existence of the studies in issue was relevant. Their contents and accuracy were not so. When the existence of something is not at issue, judicial notice may usually be taken of it.

QUICKNOTES
JUDICIAL NOTICE - The discretion of a court to recognize certain well-known facts as being true, without the necessity of a party introducing evidence to establish the truth of the fact.

UNITED STATES v. GOULD
Government (P) v. Convicted drug offender (D)
536 F.2d 216 (8th Cir. 1976).

NATURE OF CASE: Appeal from conviction for a drug offense.

FACT SUMMARY: Gould (D) challenged the trial court's action in taking judicial notice of the fact that cocaine hydrochloride was a Schedule II controlled substance and instructing the jury hearing his drug case that it had to accept this fact as conclusive.

CONCISE RULE OF LAW: Under the Federal Rules of Evidence, a court is not precluded from instructing the jury that it must accept as conclusive a "legislative" fact of which the court has taken judicial notice, i.e., a fact, truth, or pronouncement that does not change from case to case but applies universally.

FACTS: On appeal from a cocaine-related drug conviction, Gould (D) argued that the trial court had acted improperly in taking judicial notice of the fact that cocaine hydrochloride was a Schedule II controlled substance and in instructing the jury that it had to accept this fact as conclusive. At trial, there was no direct evidence to indicate that it was a derivative of coca leaves (and thus a Schedule II substance).

ISSUE: Is a federal court precluded by the Federal Rules of Evidence from instructing the jury that it must accept as conclusive a "legislative" fact of which it has taken judicial notice?

HOLDING AND DECISION: (Gibson, C.J.) No. There is nothing in the Federal Rules of Evidence to preclude a court from instructing the jury that it must accept as conclusive a "legislative" fact of which it has properly taken judicial notice. "Legislative" facts are those which involve universal facts, truths, or pronouncements that do not change from case to case, while "adjudicative" facts are those developed in a particular case. The fact that cocaine hydrochloride is derived from coca leaves is, if not common knowledge, at least a matter which is capable of certain, easily accessible and indisputably accurate verification. It is thus a proper subject of judicial notice. Furthermore, it falls within the category of "legislative" facts as opposed to "adjudicative" facts (which are the facts that relate to the parties, their activities, their properties, their businesses—and that normally go to the jury in a jury case). As such, it is not subject to Rule 201(g), which covers only adjudicative facts in calling for a jury instruction in civil cases that a judicially noticed fact is conclusive but providing that in criminal cases the jury shall be instructed that it may, but is not required to accept as conclusive, a judicially noticed fact. Thus, nothing prevents a court from instructing a jury that it must accept as conclusive the universal fact that cocaine hydrochloride is a derivative of coca. Affirmed.

EDITOR'S ANALYSIS: Not all agree with the attempted distinction between legislative and adjudicative facts. For example, Montana adopted a rule identical to Federal Rules of Evidence 201, except that instead of covering only "adjudicative facts" in terms of judicial notice, it covers "all facts" subject to judicial notice. It reasoned that the attempted distinction was confusing and could not be readily made in many situations.

QUICKNOTES

JUDICIAL NOTICE - The discretion of a court to recognize certain well-known facts as being true, without the necessity of a party introducing evidence to establish the truth of the fact.

NOTES:

CHAPTER 12
PRIVILEGES

QUICK REFERENCE RULES OF LAW

1. **Communications.** The attorney-client privilege usually provides protection for all observations resulting from privileged communication from a client leading defense counsel to physical evidence, but the original location and condition of that evidence loses the protection of the privilege if defense counsel chooses to remove the evidence to examine or test it. (People v. Meredith)

2. **Involving or Disclosing to Communicative Intermediaries.** It is essential to the attorney-client privilege that the confidential communications be made for the purpose of obtaining legal advice from a lawyer; if a client seeks advice from a nonlawyer, whether the advice sought is legal or nonlegal in nature, no attorney-client privilege exists regarding the communications. (United States v. Kovel)

3. **Leaks and Eavesdroppers.** The attorney-client privilege is waived when adequate safeguards are not employed to protect disclosure. (Suburban Sew 'N Sweep v. Swiss-Bernia)

4. **The Corporate Client.** In the case of a corporation claiming the attorney-client privilege, whether the privilege protects any particular communication must be determined on a case-by-case basis; the "control group" test does not govern. (Upjohn Co. v. United States)

5. **Client Identity.** The identity of a client is not within the protective scope of the attorney-client privilege. (In Re Grand Jury Investigation 83-2-35 (Durant))

6. **Future Crime or Fraud.** An attorney may testify regarding a client's avowed plans to commit perjury at a hearing related to that perjury. (State v. Phelps)

7. **The Psychotherapist-Patient Privilege.** Confidential communications between a psychotherapist and her patients in the course of diagnosis and treatment are protected from compelled disclosure under Rule 501 of the Federal Rules of Evidence. (Jaffee v. Redmond)

8. **Testimonial Privilege.** A criminal defendant cannot prevent his spouse from voluntarily giving testimony against him because the privilege against adverse spousal testimony belongs to the testifying spouse. (Trammel v. United States)

9. **Spousal Confidences Privilege.** Statements about past crimes made to a spouse are protected by the spousal privilege. (United States v. Estes)

10. **Drawing of Adverse Inferences.** The Fifth Amendment self-incrimination clause implicitly forbids comment by the prosecution on an accused's failure to testify, or instructions by the court that such failure is evidence of guilt. (Griffin v. California)

11. **Writings.** The contents of business records are not privileged under the Fifth Amendment. (United States v. Doe)

PEOPLE v. MEREDITH
Government (P) v. Convicted felons (D)
Cal. Sup. Ct. 631 P.2d 46 (1981).

NATURE OF CASE: Appeal from conviction for murder and robbery.

FACT SUMMARY: Scott (D), whose communications with his attorney led a defense investigator to find the murder victim's wallet (which was removed but later turned in to the police), maintained that his privilege against self-incrimination barred the investigator from testifying to the location of the wallet.

CONCISE RULE OF LAW: The attorney-client privilege usually provides protection for all observations resulting from privileged communication from a client leading defense counsel to physical evidence, but the original location and condition of that evidence loses the protection of the privilege if defense counsel chooses to remove the evidence to examine or test it.

FACTS: Scott (D) and Meredith (D) were both convicted of the first-degree murder and first-degree robbery of David Wade. When Schenk, Scott's (D) first appointed attorney visited him in jail, Scott (D) told him that the victim's wallet (which he had tried to burn) was in a plastic bag in a burn barrel behind his house. Schenk proceeded to retain an investigator, Frick, and sent Frick to find the wallet. Frick found the wallet and brought it back to Schenk, who turned it over to police after examining its contents and determining that it contained credit cards with Wade's name. Schenk only told the police that to the best of his knowledge the wallet had belonged to Wade. On appeal, Scott (D) conceded that the wallet itself was admissible, but insisted that his privilege against self-incrimination was a bar to Frick's testimony as to where the wallet had been located.

ISSUE: If defense counsel removes evidence to which he has been led by a privileged communication from his client, does the original location and condition of the evidence lose the protection of the client's privilege against self-incrimination?

HOLDING AND DECISION: (Tobriner, J.) Yes. Normally, the attorney-client privilege is not strictly limited to communications but extends to protect all observations made as a consequence of protected communication. If, therefore, a privileged communication leads defense counsel to some physical evidence, his observations thereof are insulated from revelation as long as he leaves the evidence where he discovers it. If, however, he makes the tactical decision of removing the evidence to examine or test it, the original location and condition of that evidence loses the protection of the privilege. Thus, the location of the wallet was not protected information in this case. Affirmed.

EDITOR'S ANALYSIS: As a tactical maneuver designed to prevent the jury from connecting the defendant with the party who "discovered" the evidence (as the result of privileged communications), the defense will sometimes offer to enter into a stipulation simply informing the jury as to the location or condition of the evidence. The prosecutor cannot refuse simply in the hopes of providing the opportunity for the jury to make such a connection.

QUICKNOTES
ATTORNEY-CLIENT PRIVILEGE - A doctrine precluding the admission into evidence of confidential communications between an attorney and his client made in the course of obtaining professional assistance.

NOTES:

UNITED STATES v. KOVEL
Government (P) v. Accountant (D)
296 F.2d 918 (2d Cir. 1961).

NATURE OF CASE: Appeal from a sentence for criminal contempt.

FACT SUMMARY: Kovel (D), an accountant employed by a law firm, was held in contempt for refusing to answer a grand jury inquiry regarding his client's alleged tax evasion.

CONCISE RULE OF LAW: It is essential to the attorney-client privilege that the confidential communications be made for the purpose of obtaining legal advice from a lawyer; if a client seeks advice from a nonlawyer, whether the advice sought is legal or nonlegal in nature, no attorney-client privilege exists regarding the communications.

FACTS: Kovel (D) was an accountant employed by a law firm which specialized in tax matters. During a grand jury inquiry regarding his client's alleged tax evasion, Kovel (D) refused to answer questions. He was adjudged in contempt and sentenced. Kovel (D) appealed, claiming his status as a law firm employee accorded a privilege to all communications made to him by his clients. The Government (P) argued that communications to an accountant could in no case be accorded a privilege. The facts regarding the precise nature of Kovel's (D) employment did not appear in the record.

ISSUE: Does the attorney-client privilege extend to all communications made to a nonlawyer employed by a law firm?

HOLDING AND DECISION: (Friendly, J.) No. Since there is no privilege granted to communications to nonlawyers such as accountants when operating outside a law firm, there is no reason to extend the attorney-client privilege to all communications by clients to such nonlawyers who are engaged by law firms. However, some communications may be so privileged. If the communications are made to the nonlawyer in order that he may in turn relate them to the lawyer, or in order for the nonlawyer to aid the lawyer's understanding of the client's situation so that he may offer more knowledgeable legal advice, then the communications come within the privilege. Essential to the privilege is that the communication be made in confidence for the purpose of seeking legal advice from a lawyer. If one seeks advice from a nonlawyer, whether the advice sought is legal or nonlegal in nature, no privilege exists. Here, there are insufficient facts to allow a determination regarding whether the communication to Kovel (D) by the client was made in order to obtain advice from lawyer. Vacated and remanded.

EDITOR'S ANALYSIS: *United States v. Kovel* is one of the modern authorities which applies the attorney-client privilege to communications between a lawyer and his representative, such as an accountant or investigator, although the lawyer engages him to assist the lawyer in giving legal advice, rather than merely to facilitate a communication from the client. Cases have held similarly where the one aiding the lawyer is a doctor or psychiatrist.

QUICKNOTES
ATTORNEY-CLIENT PRIVILEGE - A doctrine precluding the admission into evidence of confidential communications between an attorney and his client made in the course of obtaining professional assistance.

NOTES:

SUBURBAN SEW 'N SWEEP v. SWISS-BERNIA
Retailer (P) v. Distributor (D)
91 F.R.D. 254 (N.D. Ill. 1981).

NATURE OF CASE: Action for conspiracy and price-fixing.

FACT SUMMARY: Swiss-Bernina (P) (Swiss) contended the attorney-client privilege protected from disclosure documents intended as confidential communications yet thrown in the garbage and retrieved by Suburban (P).

CONCISE RULE OF LAW: The attorney-client privilege is waived when adequate safeguards are not employed to protect disclosure.

FACTS: Suburban (P), a retailer of sewing products distributed by Swiss (D), suspected that Swiss (D) was engaging in illegal price-fixing. Because of this, it had its employees search Swiss' (D) garbage for evidence. Over the course of two years, it retrieved several handwritten drafts of letters sent by Swiss' (D) president to its corporate counsel. In pretrial discovery, Swiss (D) attempted to exclude such documents as falling within the attorney-client privilege. The magistrate ordered the documents excluded, and Suburban (P) sought review. It contended any such privilege was waived due to lack of intended confidentiality.

ISSUE: Is the attorney-client privilege waived when adequate safeguards to disclosure are not employed?

HOLDING AND DECISION: (Leighton, J.) Yes. The attorney-client privilege is waived where adequate safeguards against disclosure are not employed. Placing the documents in the garbage indicated a lack of concern about disclosure which precludes application of the privilege. If the documents were intended to be held confidential they should have been obliterated or destroyed. Thus, the failure to do so waived the privilege. Reversed.

EDITOR'S ANALYSIS: The court rejected any argument that the documents had been obtained as the result of a Fourth Amendment violation. First, no illegal search occurs when the evidence is in the garbage because there is no reasonable expectation of privacy. Second, only government action falls under the Fourth Amendment prohibition.

QUICKNOTES
ATTORNEY-CLIENT PRIVILEGE - A doctrine precluding the admission into evidence of confidential communications between an attorney and his client made in the course of obtaining professional assistance.

NOTES:

UPJOHN CO. v. UNITED STATES
Corporation (D) v. Government (P)
449 U.S. 383 (1981).

NATURE OF CASE: Appeal from denial of privilege in tax investigation.

FACT SUMMARY: Upjohn (D) claimed the Internal Revenue Service was not entitled to production of its questionnaires to and interviews of Upjohn (D) employees concerning possibly illegal payments made by Upjohn (D), as they were privileged communications and an attorney's work product.

CONCISE RULE OF LAW: In the case of a corporation claiming the attorney-client privilege, whether the privilege protects any particular communication must be determined on a case-by-case basis; the "control group" test does not govern.

FACTS: In January 1976, independent accountants discovered that a foreign subsidiary of Upjohn (D) had made payments to or for the benefit of foreign government officials. Upjohn's (D) general counsel conducted an investigation of these "possibly illegal" payments, which included interviews of all foreign general and area managers, and various other Upjohn (D) employees, and questionnaires to the foreign managers. The IRS conducted its own investigation to determine the tax consequences of the payments. It demanded production of all Upjohn's (D) relevant files, including the questionnaires and memoranda of the interviews. Upjohn (D) claimed these were privileged and also protected as the work product of an attorney in anticipation of litigation. Upjohn (D) appealed the enforcement of the summons. The 6th Circuit affirmed to the extent that officers and employees not responsible for directing Upjohn's (D) actions in response to legal advice were not "clients" whose communications could come within the attorney-client privilege. The case was remanded to district court for a determination as to who was not within the "control group." The district court was not to consider the work product doctrine, which the Sixth Circuit found inapplicable to administrative summonses. Upjohn (D) appealed.

ISSUE: In the case of a corporation claiming the attorney-client privilege, does the privilege for any communication turn on whether the employee making the communication was responsible for directing the corporation's actions?

HOLDING AND DECISION: (Rehnquist, J.) No. The "control group" test adopted by the Sixth Circuit, which grants the attorney-client privilege to only those communications made by employees responsible for directing the corporation's actions in response to legal advice frustrates the very purpose of the privilege; this is so because it discourages communication of relevant information by employees of the client corporation to attorneys seeking to render their best legal advice to the corporate control group. Further, it invites unpredictability of application, as those whose communications receive the privilege must play a "substantial role" in directing corporate actions in response to the advice. Thus, in the case of a corporation claiming the privilege, the control group test does not govern; whether any particular communication is privileged must be determined on a case-by-case basis. Here, the communications in question were made by Upjohn (D) employees to its counsel at the direction of its officers, so that they might get advice from the counsel. Thus, these communications, the questionnaires and notes reflecting responses to interviews, are privileged. Regarding the notes which go beyond recording responses to interviews, Federal Rule 26 offers special protection to work product revealing an attorney's mental processes. While a sufficient showing of necessity can overcome protection as to tangible items and documents, a far stronger showing is required as to material revealing a lawyer's mental impressions. Here, the lesser standard was erroneously applied by the district court to the attorney's memoranda of interviews which went beyond the recording responses. Reversed and remanded.

EDITOR'S ANALYSIS: Before the Upjohn case, the weight of authority favored the control group test. A broader test that some courts employed extended the privilege to embrace any communication by an employee involving his corporate duties and made at the direction of his corporate employer. This latter test was favored by Burger in *Upjohn*, although the majority declined to formulate a standard. While avoiding some of the problems of the control group test, the broader test seemsto unduly extend the shield of privilege.

QUICKNOTES
WORK PRODUCT RULE - A doctrine excluding from discovery work performed by an attorney in preparation of litigation.

IN RE GRAND JURY INVESTIGATION 83-2-35 (DURANT)
Attorney (D) v. Government (P)
723 F.2d 447 (6th Cir. 1983).

NATURE OF CASE: Appeal from contempt citation.

FACT SUMMARY: Durant (D) contended he was precluded by the attorney-client privilege from revealing the identity of his client to the grand jury as such would expose his client to criminal prosecution.

CONCISE RULE OF LAW: The identity of a client is not within the protective scope of the attorney-client privilege.

FACTS: The FBI approached Durant (D), an attorney, and informed him it was investigating a criminal scheme involving the theft of checks made payable to IBM. Durant (D) produced a photocopy of such a check and indicated a client had used it to pay him. He was called before the grand jury and ordered to reveal the name of his client. He refused to do so on the basis that the attorney-client privilege required him not to because such would subject the client to criminal prosecution. He was cited for contempt and appealed.

ISSUE: Is the identity of a client within the protective ambit of the attorney-client privilege?

HOLDING AND DECISION: (Krupansky, J.) No. The identity of a client is not within the protective ambit of the attorney-client privilege. The basis of the privilege is the need to promote confidentiality so that clients are assured they can speak freely and openly with counsel without fear of punishment. The identity of the client does not hold the need for confidentiality upon which the privilege is based. Because no exception to the general rule on nonapplicability to client identity was shown, the privilege was not properly asserted. Affirmed.

EDITOR'S ANALYSIS: The court indicated that the proper procedural method which should have been employed by Durant (D) to test the applicability of the privilege was to demand an in camera hearing. In such a hearing he, as the party asserting the privilege, would bear the burden of establishing its application. Further, even if the general rule announced in this case applies, there are recognized exceptions. These include where the identity would implicate the client in the charge for which the legal advice was specifically sought, and where identification provides the last link in a chain of evidence used to prosecute the client.

STATE v. PHELPS
Government (P) v. Former client of attorney (D)
Ore. Ct. of App. 545 P.2d 901 (1976).

NATURE OF CASE: Appeal of evidentiary ruling in grand jury proceeding.

FACT SUMMARY: A grand jury subpoenaed Phelps' (D) attorney to testify regarding statements made to the attorney regarding plans to commit perjury.

CONCISE RULE OF LAW: An attorney may testify regarding a client's avowed plans to commit perjury at a hearing related to that perjury.

FACTS: Phelps (D) was charged with driving while intoxicated. He informed his attorney that he planned to lie on the stand. The attorney withdrew. Phelps (D) did testify. A grand jury was convened to decide whether to indict Phelps (D) for perjury. The original attorney was called to testify. Phelps (D) moved for a hearing on whether the attorney could be compelled to testify. The court held the communications privileged. The State (P) appealed.

ISSUE: May an attorney testify regarding a client's avowed plans to commit perjury, at a hearing related to that perjury?

HOLDING AND DECISION: (Schwab, C.J.) Yes. An attorney may testify regarding a client's avowed plans to commit perjury at a hearing related to that perjury. The law makes an exception to the usual rule of attorney-client confidentiality in the case of communications regarding anticipated crimes. This is based on the policy that such information has no place in the attorney-client relationship, as advising a client on committing a crime is not an attorney function. As long as the communication relates to a crime anticipated, at the time of the communication, to be done in the future, the attorney may be compelled to disclose it, even if the anticipated crime has already been committed. Such is the case here. Reversed and remanded.

EDITOR'S ANALYSIS: The future-crime exception to the attorney-client privilege is narrow. An attorney may not reveal everything in this regard. He can disclose the intention and the information necessary to prevent the crime. That is all the exception allows.

QUICKNOTES
ATTORNEY-CLIENT PRIVILEGE - A doctrine precluding the admission into evidence of confidential communications between an attorney and his client made in the course of obtaining professional assistance.

JAFFEE v. REDMOND
Executor of estate (P) v. Police officer (D)
518 U.S. 1 (1996).

NATURE OF CASE: Appeal from an award of damages in a wrongful death action.

FACT SUMMARY: Redmond (D), a police officer, underwent counseling sessions after shooting a man and sought to keep those sessions confidential in the subsequent federal civil action brought by the man's estate (P).

CONCISE RULE OF LAW: Confidential communications between a psychotherapist and her patients in the course of diagnosis and treatment are protected from compelled disclosure under Rule 501 of the Federal Rules of Evidence.

FACTS: Redmond (D), a police officer, shot and killed Allen while on duty. Jaffee (P), the executor of Allen's estate, filed a wrongful death action against Redmond (D). Following the shooting, Redmond (D) had participated in fifty counseling sessions with Beyer, a clinical social worker. Jaffee (P) sought access to Beyer's notes for use at trial. Redmond (D) asserted that the counseling sessions were confidential and privileged. The district court disagreed, but Redmond (D) and Beyer refused to comply with the discovery order to disclose the notes. At the end of the trial, the court informed the jury that the refusal to turn over the notes was not justified and that the jury should presume that the contents were unfavorable to Redmond (D). The jury awarded $545,000 in damages to Jaffee (P), but Redmond (D) appealed and prevailed. Jaffee (P) appealed the reversal of the award.

ISSUE: Are confidential communications between a psychotherapist and her patients protected from compelled disclosure?

HOLDING AND DECISION: (Stevens, J.) Yes. Confidential communications between a psychotherapist and her patients in the course of diagnosis and treatment are protected from compelled disclosure under Rule 501 of the Federal Rules of Evidence. Rule 501 of the Federal Rules of Evidence authorizes federal courts to define new privileges by interpreting common law principles in the light of reason and experience. Thus, it was recognized that the recognition of privileges would change over time. The recognition of a privilege based on a confidential relationship should be determined on a case-by-case basis, taking into account the public good that would result from allowing the privilege. Of course, privileges should still be rare because they are an exception to the general rule favoring access to all probative evidence. The psychotherapist-patient privilege is rooted in the imperative need for confidence and trust. Successful treatment for mental illnesses depends on complete openness between the psychotherapist and the patient. The mental health of the public depends in part on the confidentiality between patients and psychotherapists. In contrast, the evidentiary benefit

from denying the privilege would be modest. Patients would be chilled from expression in situations where litigation was imminent. The privilege should be extended to all licensed social workers who perform mental health treatment. Accordingly, the communications between Redmond (D) and Beyer were privileged and the trial court should not have directed the jury to make a negative inference from the refusal to divulge the contents of Beyer's notes. Reversed and remanded.

DISSENT: (Scalia, J.) While the majority goes to great lengths to show the benefit that will result from this privilege, they give short shrift to the loss of probative evidence that will cause injustice in many cases. Furthermore, the majority does not make it clear why the privilege should extend to social workers when the privilege has usually been limited to those who actually practice medicine.

EDITOR'S ANALYSIS: Prior to this decision, the court of appeals had split on this issue. Most states recognize this privilege, although most of these states extend the privilege through statute rather than common law principles. Justice Scalia also pointed out in dissent that it was not realistic to suggest that people would fail to seek therapy because the therapist might have to turn over notes by court order.

QUICKNOTES

FED. R. EVID. 501 - Provides that privilege principles shall be based on common law.

PSYCHOTHERAPIST-PATIENT PRIVILEGE - The right of a patient to refuse to reveal confidential information given during the course of a relationship with a physician entered into for the purpose of treatment.

NOTES:

TRAMMEL v. UNITED STATES
Indicted drug dealer (D) v. Government (P)
445 U.S. 40 (1980).

NATURE OF CASE: Appeal from convictions for conspiracy to import and importing heroin.

FACT SUMMARY: Trammel's (D) wife agreed to testify against her husband in return for lenient treatment for herself, but Trammel (D) argued he had the right to prevent her from testifying against him.

CONCISE RULE OF LAW: A criminal defendant cannot prevent his spouse from voluntarily giving testimony against him because the privilege against adverse spousal testimony belongs to the testifying spouse.

FACTS: In return for lenient treatment for herself, Mrs. Trammel, an unindicted co-conspirator, agreed to testify against her husband at his trial for conspiracy to import and importing heroin. The district court ruled she could testify to any act she observed during the marriage and to any communication made in the presence of a third person but not as to confidential communications between herself and her husband because they fell within the privilege attaching to confidential marital communications. On appeal, Trammel (D) contended that he was entitled to invoke the privilege against adverse spousal testimony so as to exclude the voluntary testimony of his wife. The court of appeals rejected this contention and affirmed the convictions.

ISSUE: Can a criminal defendant invoke the privilege against adverse spousal testimony so as to prevent his spouse from voluntarily offering adverse testimony against him?

HOLDING AND DECISION: (Berger, C.J.) No. Inasmuch as the privilege against adverse spousal testimony belongs solely to the testifying spouse, a criminal defendant cannot invoke the privilege to prevent his spouse from offering adverse testimony against him. The Hawkins case left the federal privilege for adverse spousal testimony where it found it at the time, thus continuing a rule which barred the testimony of one spouse against the other unless both consented. However, since that 1958 decision, support for that conception of the privilege has eroded further and the trend in state law is toward divesting the accused of the privilege to bar adverse spousal testimony. The ancient foundations for so sweeping a privilege involved a conception of the wife as her husband's chattel to do with as he wished, and they have long since disappeared. Nor is the desire to protect the marriage a valid justification for affording an accused such a privilege. If his spouse desires to testify against him, simply preventing her from doing so is not likely to save the marriage. Affirmed.

EDITOR'S ANALYSIS: The Model Code of Evidence and the Uniform Rules of Evidence completely abolished the notion of a privilege against adverse spousal testimony and limited themselves to recognizing a privilege covering confidential marital communications. Several state legislatures have followed suit.

QUICKNOTES
SPOUSAL PRIVILEGE - A common law doctrine precluding spouses from commencing actions against one another for their torts.

NOTES:

UNITED STATES v. ESTES
Government (P) v. Convicted robber (D)
793 F.2d 465 (2d Cir. 1986).

NATURE OF CASE: Appeal of conviction for bank robbery.

FACT SUMMARY: Estes (D) objected to testimony by his ex-wife regarding money stolen from his employer.

CONCISE RULE OF LAW: Statements about past crimes made to a spouse are protected by the spousal privilege.

FACTS: Estes (D) was a driver/guard for an armored car which delivered cash to banks. Estes (D) stole $55,000 from his employer. He brought the money home, and told his wife about the theft. They then secreted the funds. Subsequently, after a marital breakup, the ex-wife informed on Estes (D). The ex-wife was permitted to testify, over Estes' (D) spousal privilege objection, about the statements made when he brought home the money. Estes (D) was convicted, and he appealed.

ISSUE: Are statements about past crimes made to a spouse protected by the spousal privilege?

HOLDING AND DECISION: (Van Graafeiland, J.) Yes. Statements about past crimes made to a spouse are protected by the spousal privilege. The law, recognizing the societal importance of the marital relationship, has created the spousal privilege, which permits one spouse to prevent the testimony of the other regarding confidential communications. An exception is made in the case of ongoing criminal enterprise, as the judgment has been made by society that promoting crime is not a legitimate purpose of the marital relationship. However, statements regarding past crimes do not fall within this exception. Here, Estes' (D) statements concerned a past crime, not an ongoing enterprise. Estes (D) should have been allowed to invoke the privilege. Reversed.

EDITOR'S ANALYSIS: The scope of the spousal privilege varies greatly among the jurisdictions. At common law, a spouse could not testify against the other. No jurisdiction retains this, but the extent to which a spouse can testify against another is quite unsettled. For instance, some jurisdictions only allow the privilege to be invoked if the couple is still married.

NOTES:

QUICKNOTES
SPOUSAL PRIVILEGE - A common law doctrine precluding spouses from commencing actions against one another for their torts.

GRIFFIN v. CALIFORNIA
Convicted murderer (D) v. State (P)
380 U.S. 609 (1965).

NATURE OF CASE: Certiorari from a murder conviction.

FACT SUMMARY: Griffin (D), during his trial for first-degree murder, did not testify on the issue of his guilt, and both the prosecutor and judge subsequently commented on this failure to the jury, before it convicted him.

CONCISE RULE OF LAW: The Fifth Amendment self-incrimination clause implicitly forbids comment by the prosecution on an accused's failure to testify, or instructions by the court that such failure is evidence of guilt.

FACTS: Griffin (D) refused to testify at his trial for first-degree murder, invoking the Fifth Amendment privilege against self-incrimination. Before the jury deliberated on the issue of guilt, the prosecutor commented on this failure to testify and suggested that guilt should be inferred therefrom. During instructions to the jury, the court stated that if Griffin (D) failed to explain facts within his knowledge which tended to indicate his guilt, then the jury could take that failure as "tending to indicate the truth of such evidence," but that such failure alone does not by itself "warrant an inference of guilt." Upon conviction, and affirmance of that conviction by the California Supreme Court, Griffin (D) brought a petition for certiorari to this court.

ISSUE: Does comment by a judge or prosecutor on an accused's failure to testify violate his Fifth Amendment privilege against self-incrimination?

HOLDING AND DECISION: (Douglas, J.) Yes. The Fifth Amendment self-incriminating clause forbids comment by the prosecution on an accused's failure to testify, or instructions by the court that such failure is evidence of guilt. Such comment by the prosecution or court is a "remnant of the inquisitorial system of criminal justice which the Fifth Amendment protects against." Such comment penalizes the exercise of a constitutional privilege to refrain from self-incrimination and, as such, cannot be allowed. It may be true that there is a natural inference of guilt from a failure to testify as to facts within the knowledge of an accused, but the jury must make this inference on its own without comment from the court. Here, therefore, Griffin's (D) conviction must be reversed.

DISSENT: (Stewart, J.) The Court in this case stretches the concept of compulsion beyond all reasonable bounds, and whatever compulsion may exist derives from Griffin's (D) choice not to testify, not from any comment by court or counsel. The California comment rule is not a coercive device which impairs the right against self-incrimination, but rather a means of articulating

and bringing into the light of rational discussion a fact inescapably impressed on the jury's consciousness. The California procedure is not only designed to protect the defendant against unwarranted inferences which might be drawn by an uninformed jury; it is also an attempt by the State (P) to recognize and articulate what it believes to be the natural probative force of certain facts.

EDITOR'S ANALYSIS: This case illustrates the rule applicable to "direct comment" on an accused's failure to "testify." Note, however, that it does not prevent a prosecutor from commenting on an accused's "failure to offer evidence" on critical aspects of the case. It has been held that a court's comment that an accused's "failure to explain" possession of recently stolen property should be considered in determining whether he knew the goods were stolen, does not violate Griffin (Barnes v. U.S.). Of course, what is considered permissible depends upon the wording of the prosecutor's comments. If he emphasizes an accused's failure to present other evidence instead of the fact that he "personally" offered no explanation, there is probably no violation of Griffin. Note further that Griffin does not prevent a prosecutor from commenting to a jury upon an accused's "refusal to submit to reasonable tests or examinations," the results of which would have been admissible on the issue of guilt or innocence. Note, finally, that Griffin does prevent counsel for one of several co-defendants from commenting on the failure of other co-defendants to testify.

QUICKNOTES

CERTIORARI - A discretionary writ issued by a superior court to an inferior court in order to review the lower court's decisions; the Supreme Court's writ ordering such review.

FIFTH AMENDMENT - Provides that no person shall be compelled to serve as a witness against himself, or be subject to trial for the same offense twice, or be deprived of life, liberty, or property without due process of law.

SELF-INCRIMINATION - A privilege guaranteed by the Fifth Amendment to the federal Constitution in a criminal proceeding for communications made by an accused and protecting an accused or witness from having to give testimony that may incriminate himself.

UNITED STATES v. DOE
Government (P) v. Businessman (D)
465 U.S. 605 (1984).

NATURE OF CASE: Review of order quashing a subpoena.

FACT SUMMARY: Doe (D), recipient of a grand jury subpoena of business records, contended the contents thereof were privileged under the Fifth Amendment.

CONCISE RULE OF LAW: The contents of business records are not privileged under the Fifth Amendment.

FACTS: Doe (D) was investigated by a grand jury, pursuant to fraud allegations. The jury issued a subpoena for certain business records he had prepared. Doe (D) moved to quash, contending that the contents thereof were privileged by the Fifth Amendment's Self-Incrimination Clause. The district court granted the motion, and the Fifth Circuit affirmed. The Supreme Court granted certiorari.

ISSUE: Are the contents of business records privileged under the Fifth Amendment?

HOLDING AND DECISION: (Powell, J.) No. The contents of business records are not privileged under the Fifth Amendment. The Fifth Amendment protects an individual against compelled testimony. When a person has freely created records, whether they are incriminating or not is irrelevant for Fifth Amendment purposes. The absence of compulsion in the creation of the records takes the contents of the records out of the ambit of the Fifth Amendment. [The Court went on to rule that, under some circumstances, the act of producing such records could constitute a Fifth Amendment violation. The case was remanded to the district court to give the government (P) the opportunity to request immunity for Doe (D) as to the act of producing the records.] Affirmed in part; reversed in part.

CONCURRENCE: (O'Connor, J.) The contents of private papers may never be protected by the Fifth Amendment.

CONCURRENCE AND DISSENT: (Marshall, J.) The Court did not have to reach the issue of contents as the production aspect of the case was sufficient for the Court to do as it did. Further, there are certain documents no person ought to be compelled to produce.

CONCURRENCE AND DISSENT: (Stevens, J.) The only issue in this case was production, not the privileged or nonprivileged status of the contents of business records.

EDITOR'S ANALYSIS: The Fifth Amendment textually prohibits testimony regarding oneself. Literally speaking, producing a record is not tantamount to testifying. However, in producing records, an individual does affirm them as being that requested, and this involves an element of testimony.

QUICKNOTES

CERTIORARI - A discretionary writ issued by a superior court to an inferior court in order to review the lower court's decisions; the Supreme Court's writ ordering such review.

FIFTH AMENDMENT - Provides that no person shall be compelled to serve as a witness against himself, or be subject to trial for the same offense twice, or be deprived of life, liberty, or property without due process of law.

NOTES:

CHAPTER 13
FOUNDATIONAL EVIDENCE, AUTHENTICATION

QUICK REFERENCE RULES OF LAW

1. **Tangible Objects.** Federal Rule of Evidence 901 provides that the requirement of authentication as a condition precedent to admissibility is satisfied by evidence sufficient to support a finding that the matter in question is what its proponent claims. (United States v. Johnson)

2. **Tangible Objects.** Tangible evidence will not be made inadmissible merely because one custodian thereof fails to testify. (United States v. Howard-Arias)

3. **Writings.** A letter may be authenticated by the names contained therein. (United States v. Bagaric)

4. **Tape Recordings.** Participant testimony regarding a transaction electronically recorded may suffice to lay a foundation for admittance of the recording into evidence. (United States v. Biggins)

5. **Telephone Conversations.** A statement made over the telephone may be excluded from evidence if the caller's identity cannot be established. (United States v. Pool)

UNITED STATES v. JOHNSON
Government (P) v. Convicted felon (D)
637 F.2d 1224 (9th Cir. 1980).

NATURE OF CASE: Appeal from an assault conviction.

FACT SUMMARY: Johnson (D) contended the trial court erred in admitting into evidence an ax which was not properly authenticated by the prosecution.

CONCISE RULE OF LAW: Federal Rule of Evidence 901 provides that the requirement of authentication as a condition precedent to admissibility is satisfied by evidence sufficient to support a finding that the matter in question is what its proponent claims.

FACTS: Johnson (D) was arrested for an attack with an ax on a victim named Papse. At trial, the prosecution called Papse as a witness and attempted to authenticate an ax as the weapon of assault. Papse identified the ax; however, he could not distinguish that ax from any other ax, and could not identify specific characteristics of this ax which could tie it to the incident. Johnson (D) contended this was insufficient authentication to allow the ax into evidence. The trial court allowed the ax into evidence, and Johnson (D) was convicted. He appealed, contending the trial court erred in admitting the ax.

ISSUE: Is the requirement of authentication as a condition precedent to admissibility satisfied by evidence sufficient to support a finding that the matter in question is what its proponent claims?

HOLDING AND DECISION: (Williams, J.) Yes. Federal Rule of Evidence 901 provides that the requirement of authentication as a condition precedent to admissibility is satisfied by evidence sufficient to support a finding that the matter in question is what its proponent claims. In this case, the prosecution merely had to provide sufficient evidence that the ax produced in court was the ax used in the incident. It was not required to establish that the witness could distinguish this ax from any other ax, nor was it required to have the witness testify as to the specific characteristics of this ax. While the identification may not have been entirely free from doubt, the witness did state that he was pretty sure this was the weapon that had been used against him. He further testified that he was personally familiar with the particular ax because he had used it in the past. Thus, a reasonable juror could have found that this ax was the weapon allegedly used in the assault. Thus, there was no abuse of discretion in the trial court's ruling that proper authentication was made. As a result, the conviction must stand.

EDITOR'S ANALYSIS: This case illustrates that in federal court, as well as in most state courts, the initial condition precedent to allowing materials into evidence is proper authentication. The requirement is that the proponent of the evidence present sufficient evidence that the particular material is what it purports to be. When dealing with documentary evidence, a witness familiar with either the preparation of the document, or familiar with the handwriting of the person creating the document is usually sufficient for that witness to testify that the particular documentary evidence is what it purports to be. Authentication does not establish the weight to be given to the particular piece of evidence; it merely allows the material into evidence so that the trier of fact can then weigh its reliability against any countervailing evidence. Usually when dealing with evidence of either a documentary or other nature, the chain of custody of the evidence is an important issue to be established by the proponent. A failure to account for the chain of possession of evidence from the incident involved to the trial may lead to its exclusion.

QUICKNOTES

AUTHENTICATION (OF DOCUMENTARY EVIDENCE) - The validity of documentary evidence that must be established prior to its admission into evidence, usually by showing that a document is that it purports to be.

FED. R. EVID. § 901 – Federal Rule of Evidence setting forth the means of compliance with the requirement of authentification as a condition precedent to admissibility.

NOTES:

UNITED STATES v. HOWARD-ARIAS
Government (P) v. Convicted drug dealer (D)
679 F.2d 363 (4th Cir. 1982).

NATURE OF CASE: Appeal of conviction for drug-related offenses.

NOTES:

FACT SUMMARY: Howard-Arias (D) contended that seized contraband could not be introduced into evidence because one of the individuals involved in the "chain of custody" did not testify.

CONCISE RULE OF LAW: Tangible evidence will not be made inadmissible merely because one custodian thereof fails to testify.

FACTS: A large amount of marijuana was found on a disabled ship on which Howard-Arias (D) had been a crew member. The U.S. Coast Guard took both Howard-Arias (D) and the marijuana into custody. Howard-Arias (D) objected, as one of the persons forming the "chain of custody" did not testify regarding authentication. The district court overruled the objection, and Howard-Arias (D) was convicted. He appealed.

ISSUE: Will tangible evidence be made inadmissible merely because one custodian thereof fails to testify?

HOLDING AND DECISION: (Per curiam) No. Tangible evidence will not be made inadmissible merely because one custodian thereof fails to testify. Real evidence must be authenticated prior to admission. This is to ensure that the proffered item is in fact that which it is purported to be. The question is whether the authentication testimony is sufficiently complete so as to convince the court that the original item was, in fact, what was offered. This is a matter for the trial court's discretion; there is no rule that every custodian of the item need testify. Here, it is well within the court's discretion to find contraband authenticated. Affirmed.

EDITOR'S ANALYSIS: Not all courts have been as lenient with authentication as this one. Many courts have rejected evidence due to a failure to produce each custodian thereof. Because of the reasonable doubt standard in criminal cases, the issue arises most often in criminal cases.

QUICKNOTES
AUTHENTICATION (OF DOCUMENTARY EVIDENCE) - The validity of documentary evidence that must be established prior to its admission into evidence, usually by showing that a document is that it purports to be.

UNITED STATES v. BAGARIC
Government (P) v. Convicted felon (D)
706 F.2d 42 (2d Cir. 1983).

NATURE OF CASE: Appeal under the Racketeer Influenced and Corrupt Organizations Act.

FACT SUMMARY: A letter incriminating as to Logarusic (D) was deemed authentic because it was replete with references to Logarusic's (D) circle of conspirators.

CONCISE RULE OF LAW: A letter may be authenticated by the names contained therein.

FACTS: Logarusic (D), Bagaric (D), Markich (D), Primorac (D), Sudar (D) and Ljubas (D) were indicted under the RICO Act. At trial, the Government (P) sought to introduce a letter found during a search of Logarusic's (D) home. The letter contained incriminating information. It was addressed to Logarusic (D) from Bagaric (D) and contained numerous references to the circle of indicted conspirators, including aliases. Over Logarusic's (D) foundational objection, the letter was admitted into evidence. Logarusic (D) was convicted, and he appealed, arguing that the letter could not be authenticated by the names that appeared in it.

ISSUE: May a letter be authenticated by names contained therein?

HOLDING AND DECISION: (Kaufman, J.) Yes. A letter may be authenticated by names contained therein. The requirement of authentication, per Fed. R. Evid. 901(a), is satisfied by evidence sufficient to support a finding that the matter is what the proponent claims it is. Where the evidence at issue is a letter, the names contained therein can be sufficient to demonstrate this. Here, the names in the letter of the various defendants give ample support to the contention that the letter was in fact a correspondence from Bagaric (D) to Logarusic (D). Affirmed.

EDITOR'S ANALYSIS: The requirement of authentication was rather strict at common law. The proof that the connection between proffered evidence and a party did, in fact, exist had to be convincing. Today, under Fed. R. Evid. 901(b), the evidence of authentication need only be sufficient to support an authentication finding.

QUICKNOTES

RICO - Racketeer Influenced and Corrupt Organization laws; federal and state statutes enacted for the purpose of prosecuting organized crime.

NOTES:

UNITED STATES v. BIGGINS
Government (P) v. Convicted drug dealer (D)
551 F.2d 64 (5th Cir. 1977).

NATURE OF CASE: Appeal of conviction for selling heroin.

FACT SUMMARY: An incriminating tape recording of a transaction involving Biggins (D) was admitted after the Government's (P) witnesses testified it accurately memorialized the event.

CONCISE RULE OF LAW: Participant testimony regarding a transaction electronically recorded may suffice to lay a foundation for admittance of the recording into evidence.

FACTS: Biggins (D) was "set-up" by Government (P) agents Lydes and Wells to sell heroin to Wells. The transaction was recorded by audiotape. At trial, the Government (P) sought to introduce the tape. Testimony revealed that the operator of the recording equipment was of questionable knowledgeability, and the post-recording techniques may have been substandard. Nonetheless, the district court admitted the tape after Lydes and Wells testified that the tape was accurate. Biggins' (D) foundation objection was overruled, and he appealed his conviction.

ISSUE: May participant testimony regarding a transaction electronically recorded suffice to lay a foundation for admittance of the recording into evidence?

HOLDING AND DECISION: (Goldberg, J.) Yes. Participant testimony regarding a transaction electronically recorded may suffice to lay a foundation for admittance of the recording into evidence. Because inherent problems with the reliability of electronic recordings, courts have taken care to ensure that a criminal defendant will not be prejudiced by admission of a recording that may not accurately portray what transpired. A variety of tests have been adopted, all calculated to ensure that the recording is accurate. Since accuracy is the key to whether a recording may be admitted, a trial court should be allowed to admit a recording when the circumstances demonstrate such accuracy. Even if the recording process was suspect, if testimonial evidence indicates it is accurate, exclusion should not be mandated. Here, two Government (P) agents testified that the tape was in fact accurate. The trial court did not abuse its discretion in admitting the tape. Affirmed.

EDITOR'S ANALYSIS: A very influential case regarding admissibility of electronic recordings is *United States v. McKeever*, 169 F. Supp. 426 (S.D.N.Y 1958), where a strict seven-part test for admissibility is defined. The court here expressly rejected the test, concentrating instead on overall accuracy.

UNITED STATES v. POOL
Government (P) v. Convicted drug smuggler (D)
660 F.2d 547 (5th Cir. 1981).

NATURE OF CASE: Appeal of conviction for marijuana importation.

FACT SUMMARY: Loye (D) was convicted after a Government (P) agent who had never met Loye (D) received a telephone call in which an individual identifying himself as Loye (D) made incriminating statements.

CONCISE RULE OF LAW: A statement made over the telephone may be excluded from evidence if the caller's identity cannot be established.

FACTS: While doing an undercover investigation of a drug smuggling operation, DEA agent Starratt received a telephone call from an individual identifying himself as "Chip," a nickname used throughout the investigation. Starratt had never met Loye (D), nor theretofore heard his voice. Based partially on these statements, Loye (D) was indicted and convicted. He appealed.

ISSUE: May a statement made over the telephone be excluded from evidence if the caller's identity cannot be established?

HOLDING AND DECISION: (Hill, J.) Yes. A statement made over the telephone may be excluded from evidence if the caller's identity cannot be established. For a telephone call to be admitted into evidence, at least a prima facie case must be made regarding authentication of the caller's identity. No particular type of proof is determinative. However, a mere self-identification by the caller, unaccompanied by anything else, is sufficient. Here, self-identification was all that was offered to authenticate, as Starratt had no personal knowledge as to Loye's (D) voice characteristics. This was insufficient authentication. Reversed.

EDITOR'S ANALYSIS: Numerous possible ways of authenticating a telephone call can be envisioned. Recording the caller's voice is a possibility. Another possibility would be the recipient of the call being familiar with the caller. Whether any of these would suffice in any given situation would depend on the facts of the case.

14

CHAPTER 14
THE "BEST EVIDENCE" DOCTRINE

QUICK REFERENCE RULES OF LAW

1. **Defining a "Writing Recording, or Photograph".** The Best Evidence Rule covers writings and provides that the original writing must be produced unless it is shown to be unavailable for some reason other than the serious fault of the proponent. (United States v. Duffy)

2. **Best Evidence Doctrine in Operation.** The Best Evidence Rule is limited to cases where the contents of a writing are to be proved. (Meyers v. United States)

3. **Production of Original Excused.** Where material records are not shown to be unavailable, the records rather than summaries thereof must be introduced. (Sylvania Electric Products v. Flanagan)

UNITED STATES v. DUFFY
Government (P) v. Convicted thief (D)
454 F.2d 809 (5th Cir. 1972).

NATURE OF CASE: Appeal from a conviction for transporting a stolen vehicle in interstate commerce.

FACT SUMMARY: Two witnesses testified that a shirt found in a suitcase in the car Duffy (D) was accused of stealing had the laundry mark "D-U-F," but Duffy (D) objected to the testimony and claimed the Best Evidence Rule required that the Government (P) produce the shirt.

CONCISE RULE OF LAW: The Best Evidence Rule covers writings and provides that the original writing must be produced unless it is shown to be unavailable for some reason other than the serious fault of the proponent.

FACTS: A car that had been brought into the Florida body shop where Duffy (D) worked disappeared over the same weekend he did. Both were later found in California. Duffy (D) was convicted of transporting a motor vehicle in interstate commerce knowing it to have been stolen. On appeal, he complained of error in the admission of certain evidence. Specifically, two witnesses had testified that the trunk of the stolen car had contained two suitcases when found, and that in one of the suitcases was a white shirt with the laundry mark "D-U-F." Duffy (D) argued that the Best Evidence Rule required the United States (D) to produce the shirt itself, because the laundry mark made it proper to treat the shirt as a "writing."

ISSUE: Does the Best Evidence Rule cover writings only?

HOLDING AND DECISION: (Wisdom, J.) Yes. Only writings are covered by the Best Evidence Rule. According to McCormick, the Rule, as it exists today, may be stated as follows: "[I]n proving the terms of a writing, where such terms are material, the original writing must be produced unless it is shown to be unavailable for some reason other than the serious fault of the proponent." When, as in this case, the disputed evidence is an object bearing a mark or inscription, and is, therefore, a chattel and a writing, the trial judge has discretion to treat the evidence as a chattel or as a writing. Here, the inscription on the shirt was simple and there was little danger it could not be accurately remembered. Furthermore, its terms were by no means central or critical to the case, the shirt being only collateral evidence of the crime and only one piece of evidence in a substantial case against Duffy (D). Thus, the policy considerations behind the Rule are not present and the judge acted properly in treating the shirt as chattel instead of as a writing. Affirmed.

EDITOR'S ANALYSIS: A number of courts agree with Wigmore and McCormick that the trial judge should have the discretion to decide whether the Best Evidence Rule should be applied in any individual case involving an inscribed chattel. However, the Uniform Rules of Evidence adopt the strident position that any object carrying an inscription should be treated as a "writing."

QUICKNOTES
BEST EVIDENCE RULE - An evidentiary rule requiring that an original document be introduced if possible; secondary evidence is only admissible after proof that the original was lost or destroyed through no fault of the proponent.

NOTES:

MEYERS v. UNITED STATES
Businessman (D) v. Government (P)
171 F.2d 800 (D.C. Cir. 1948).

NATURE OF CASE: Appeal from conviction for perjury.

FACT SUMMARY: Meyers (D) contended that the United States (P) violated the Best Evidence Rule by allowing testimony as to what was contained in a transcript.

CONCISE RULE OF LAW: The Best Evidence Rule is limited to cases where the contents of a writing are to be proved.

FACTS: Lamarre testified before a committee of the United States Senate investigating fraud and corruption in the conduct of World War II that he, and not General Bennett Meyers (D), was the actual owner of Aviation Electric Corporation which had held numerous lucrative contracts with the Army Air Force. Meyers (D) was a deputy chief procurement officer for the Army Air Force. Lamarre was indicted for perjury, and Meyers (D) was indicted for suborning the perjury of Lamarre. During the trial, William P. Rogers, the chief counsel to the senatorial committee, was permitted to testify as to what Lamarre had sworn to the subcommittee. Later in the trial, the Government (P) introduced in evidence a stenographic transcript of Lamarre's testimony at the Senate hearing. After being convicted of the charges, Meyers (D) appealed, arguing that the trial court violated the Best Evidence Rule by allowing Rogers to testify, when the transcript of Lamarre's testimony was actually the best evidence of what had been stated before the subcommittee.

ISSUE: Is the Best Evidence Rule limited to cases where the contents of a writing are to be proved?

HOLDING AND DECISION: (Miller,J.) Yes. The Best Evidence Rule is limited to cases where the contents of a writing are to be proved. Here, there was no attempt to prove the contents of a writing; the issue was what Lamarre had said, not what the transcript contained. The transcript made from shorthand notes of his testimony was evidence of what he had said, but it was not the only admissible evidence concerning it. Rogers' testimony was equally competent and admissible whether given before or after the transcript was received in evidence. Statements alleged to be perjurious may be proved by any person who heard them, as well as by a reporter who recorded them in shorthand. Affirmed.

DISSENT: (Prettyman, J.) The testimony given by Lamarre before the Senate Committee was presented to the jury at trial in so unfair and prejudicial a fashion as to constitute reversible error. Rogers did not purport to be absolute in his reproduction but merely recited his unrefreshed recollection, and his recollection on each of the alleged incidents of perjury bears a striking resemblance to the succinct summations in the indictment. It is obvious that what Rogers gave as substance was an essence of his own distillation and not an attempt to reproduce the whole of Lamarre's testimony.

EDITOR'S ANALYSIS: The Federal Rules state that: "To prove the content of a writing, recording, or photograph, the original writing, recording, or photograph is required, except as otherwise provided in (the Federal) rules or by Act of Congress." See Fed. R. Evid. 1002.

QUICKNOTES

BEST EVIDENCE RULE – An evidentiary rule requiring that an original document be introduced if possible; secondary evidence is only admissible after proof that the original was lost or destroyed through no fault of the proponent.

FED. R. EVID. 1002 – Federal Rule of Evidence codifying the common law Best Evidence Rule.

NOTES:

SYLVANIA ELECTRIC PRODUCTS v. FLANAGAN
Electric company (D) v. Employee (P)
352 F.2d 1005 (1st Cir. 1965).

NATURE OF CASE: Appeal of award of damages for breach of contract.

FACT SUMMARY: Flanagan (P) was permitted to introduce a summary of certain material records rather than the records themselves, without showing the unavailability thereof.

CONCISE RULE OF LAW: Where material records are not shown to be unavailable, the records rather than summaries thereof must be introduced.

FACTS: Flanagan (P) performed certain excavation work for Sylvania Electric Products (D). At the end of the project, Sylvania (D) disputed the amount of hours that Flanagan (P) had devoted to the project. The contract called for Flanagan (P) to be paid on an hourly basis. Flanagan (P) sued for breach of contract. At trial, Flanagan (P) introduced a summary he had made of certain records which purported to show the amount of time spent on the project. Sylvania (D) objected based on the Best Evidence Rule. When asked by the court where the originals were, Flanagan (P) replied he had some at home. He never produced the originals, but the summary was admitted anyway. The jury awarded Flanagan (P) over $25,000, and Sylvania (D) appealed.

ISSUE: Where material records are not shown to be unavailable, must the records rather than summaries thereof be introduced?

HOLDING AND DECISION: (McEntee, J.) Yes. Where material records are not shown to be unavailable, the records rather than summaries thereof must be introduced. It is well settled that the best evidence that is obtainable in the circumstances of the case must be adduced to prove any disputed fact. The more central the records are to the issue of the case, the more strictly this rule will be enforced. This has been interpreted to require originals when available. Here, the records which were not produced purported to prove the number of hours worked, which was the central issue of the case. No showing of unavailability was made. This was error on the part of the district court. Reversed.

EDITOR'S ANALYSIS: The Best Evidence Rule often comes into play with the hearsay rule. Such records are often business related. The business record exception to the hearsay rule must often be invoked to permit the records required by the Best Evidence Rule.

BREACH OF CONTRACT - Unlawful failure by a party to perform its obligations pursuant to contract.

NOTES:

GLOSSARY
COMMON LATIN WORDS AND PHRASES ENCOUNTERED IN THE LAW

A FORTIORI: Because one fact exists or has been proven, therefore a second fact that is related to the first fact must also exist.

A PRIORI: From the cause to the effect. A term of logic used to denote that when one generally accepted truth is shown to be a cause, another particular effect must necessarily follow.

AB INITIO: From the beginning; a condition which has existed throughout, as in a marriage which was void ab initio.

ACTUS REUS: The wrongful act; in criminal law, such action sufficient to trigger criminal liability.

AD VALOREM: According to value; an ad valorem tax is imposed upon an item located within the taxing jurisdiction calculated by the value of such item.

AMICUS CURIAE: Friend of the court. Its most common usage takes the form of an amicus curiae brief, filed by a person who is not a party to an action but is nonetheless allowed to offer an argument supporting his legal interests.

ARGUENDO: In arguing. A statement, possibly hypothetical, made for the purpose of argument, is one made arguendo.

BILL QUIA TIMET: A bill to quiet title (establish ownership) to real property.

BONA FIDE: True, honest, or genuine. May refer to a person's legal position based on good faith or lacking notice of fraud (such as a bona fide purchaser for value) or to the authenticity of a particular document (such as a bona fide last will and testament).

CAUSA MORTIS: With approaching death in mind. A gift causa mortis is a gift given by a party who feels certain that death is imminent.

CAVEAT EMPTOR: Let the buyer beware. This maxim is reflected in the rule of law that a buyer purchases at his own risk because it is his responsibility to examine, judge, test, and otherwise inspect what he is buying.

CERTIORARI: A writ of review. Petitions for review of a case by the United States Supreme Court are most often done by means of a writ of certiorari.

CONTRA: On the other hand. Opposite. Contrary to.

CORAM NOBIS: Before us; writs of error directed to the court that originally rendered the judgment.

CORAM VOBIS: Before you; writs of error directed by an appellate court to a lower court to correct a factual error.

CORPUS DELICTI: The body of the crime; the requisite elements of a crime amounting to objective proof that a crime has been committed.

CUM TESTAMENTO ANNEXO, ADMINISTRATOR (ADMINISTRATOR C.T.A.): With will annexed; an administrator c.t.a. settles an estate pursuant to a will in which he is not appointed.

DE BONIS NON, ADMINISTRATOR (ADMINISTRATOR D.B.N.): Of goods not administered; an administrator d.b.n. settles a partially settled estate.

DE FACTO: In fact; in reality; actually. Existing in fact but not officially approved or engendered.

DE JURE: By right; lawful. Describes a condition that is legitimate "as a matter of law," in contrast to the term "de facto," which connotes something existing in fact but not legally sanctioned or authorized. For example, de facto segregation refers to segregation brought about by housing patterns, etc., whereas de jure segregation refers to segregation created by law.

DE MINIMUS: Of minimal importance; insignificant; a trifle; not worth bothering about.

DE NOVO: Anew; a second time; afresh. A trial de novo is a new trial held at the appellate level as if the case originated there and the trial at a lower level had not taken place.

DICTA: Generally used as an abbreviated form of obiter dicta, a term describing those portions of a judicial opinion incidental or not necessary to resolution of the specific question before the court. Such nonessential statements and remarks are not considered to be binding precedent.

DUCES TECUM: Refers to a particular type of writ or subpoena requesting a party or organization to produce certain documents in their possession.

EN BANC: Full bench. Where a court sits with all justices present rather than the usual quorum.

EX PARTE: For one side or one party only. An ex parte proceeding is one undertaken for the benefit of only one party, without notice to, or an appearance by, an adverse party.

EX POST FACTO: After the fact. An ex post facto law is a law that retroactively changes the consequences of a prior act.

EX REL.: Abbreviated form of the term ex relatione, meaning, upon relation or information. When the state brings an action in which it has no interest against an individual at the instigation of one who has a private interest in the matter.

FORUM NON CONVENIENS: Inconvenient forum. Although a court may have jurisdiction over the case, the action should be tried in a more conveniently located court, one to which parties and witnesses may more easily travel, for example.

GUARDIAN AD LITEM: A guardian of an infant as to litigation, appointed to represent the infant and pursue his/her rights.

HABEAS CORPUS: You have the body. The modern writ of habeas corpus is a writ directing that a person (body) being detained (such as a prisoner) be brought before the court so that the legality of his detention can be judicially ascertained.

IN CAMERA: In private, in chambers. When a hearing is held before a judge in his chambers or when all spectators are excluded from the courtroom.

IN FORMA PAUPERIS: In the manner of a pauper. A party who proceeds in forma pauperis because of his poverty is one who is allowed to bring suit without liability for costs.

INFRA: Below, under. A word referring the reader to a later part of a book. (The opposite of supra.)

IN LOCO PARENTIS: In the place of a parent.

IN PARI DELICTO: Equally wrong; a court of equity will not grant requested relief to an applicant who is in pari delicto, or as much at fault in the transactions giving rise to the controversy as is the opponent of the applicant.

IN PARI MATERIA: On like subject matter or upon the same matter. Statutes relating to the same person or things are said to be in pari materia. It is a general rule of statutory construction that such statutes should be construed together, i.e., looked at as if they together constituted one law.

IN PERSONAM: Against the person. Jurisdiction over the person of an individual.

IN RE: In the matter of. Used to designate a proceeding involving an estate or other property.

IN REM: A term that signifies an action against the res, or thing. An action in rem is basically one that is taken directly against property, as distinguished from an action in personam, i.e., against the person.

INTER ALIA: Among other things. Used to show that the whole of a statement, pleading, list, statute, etc., has not been set forth in its entirety.

INTER PARTES: Between the parties. May refer to contracts, conveyances or other transactions having legal significance.

INTER VIVOS: Between the living. An inter vivos gift is a gift made by a living grantor, as distinguished from bequests contained in a will, which pass upon the death of the testator.

IPSO FACTO: By the mere fact itself.

JUS: Law or the entire body of law.

LEX LOCI: The law of the place; the notion that the rights of parties to a legal proceeding are governed by the law of the place where those rights arose.

MALUM IN SE: Evil or wrong in and of itself; inherently wrong. This term describes an act that is wrong by its very nature, as opposed to one which would not be wrong but for the fact that there is a specific legal prohibition against it (malum prohibitum).

MALUM PROHIBITUM: Wrong because prohibited, but not inherently evil. Used to describe something that is wrong because it is expressly forbidden by law but that is not in and of itself evil, e.g., speeding.

MANDAMUS: We command. A writ directing an official to take a certain action.

MENS REA: A guilty mind; a criminal intent. A term used to signify the mental state that accompanies a crime or other prohibited act. Some crimes require only a general mens rea (general intent to do the prohibited act), but others, like assault with intent to murder, require the existence of a specific mens rea.

MODUS OPERANDI: Method of operating; generally refers to the manner or style of a criminal in committing crimes, admissible in appropriate cases as evidence of the identity of a defendant.

NEXUS: A connection to.

NISI PRIUS: A court of first impression. A nisi prius court is one where issues of fact are tried before a judge or jury.

N.O.V. (NON OBSTANTE VEREDICTO): Notwithstanding the verdict. A judgment n.o.v. is a judgment given in favor of one party despite the fact that a verdict was returned in favor of the other party, the justification being that the verdict either had no reasonable support in fact or was contrary to law.

NUNC PRO TUNC: Now for then. This phrase refers to actions that may be taken and will then have full retroactive effect.

PENDENTE LITE: Pending the suit; pending litigation underway.

PER CAPITA: By head; beneficiaries of an estate, if they take in equal shares, take per capita.

PER CURIAM: By the court; signifies an opinion ostensibly written "by the whole court" and with no identified author.

PER SE: By itself, in itself; inherently.

PER STIRPES: By representation. Used primarily in the law of wills to describe the method of distribution where a person, generally because of death, is unable to take that which is left to him by the will of another, and therefore his heirs divide such property between them rather than take under the will individually.

PRIMA FACIE: On its face, at first sight. A prima facie case is one that is sufficient on its face, meaning that the evidence supporting it is adequate to establish the case until contradicted or overcome by other evidence.

PRO TANTO: For so much; as far as it goes. Often used in eminent domain cases when a property owner receives partial payment for his land without prejudice to his right to bring suit for the full amount he claims his land to be worth.

QUANTUM MERUIT: As much as he deserves. Refers to recovery based on the doctrine of unjust enrichment in those cases in which a party has rendered valuable services or furnished materials that were accepted and enjoyed by another under circumstances that would reasonably notify the recipient that the rendering party expected to be paid. In essence, the law implies a contract to pay the reasonable value of the services or materials furnished.

QUASI: Almost like; as if; nearly. This term is essentially used to signify that one subject or thing is almost analogous to another but that material differences between them do exist. For example, a quasi-criminal proceeding is one that is not strictly criminal but shares enough of the same characteristics to require some of the same safeguards (e.g., procedural due process must be followed in a parol hearing).

QUID PRO QUO: Something for something. In contract law, the consideration, something of value, passed between the parties to render the contract binding.

RES GESTAE: Things done; in evidence law, this principle justifies the admission of a statement that would otherwise be hearsay when it is made so closely to the event in question as to be said to be a part of it, or with such spontaneity as not to have the possibility of falsehood.

RES IPSA LOQUITUR: The thing speaks for itself. This doctrine gives rise to a rebuttable presumption of negligence when the instrumentality causing the injury was within the exclusive control of the defendant, and the injury was one that does not normally occur unless a person has been negligent.

RES JUDICATA: A matter adjudged. Doctrine which provides that once a court of competent jurisdiction has rendered a final judgment or decree on the merits, that judgment or decree is conclusive upon the parties to the case and prevents them from engaging in any other litigation on the points and issues determined therein.

RESPONDEAT SUPERIOR: Let the master reply. This doctrine holds the master liable for the wrongful acts of his servant (or the principal for his agent) in those cases in which the servant (or agent) was acting within the scope of his authority at the time of the injury.

STARE DECISIS: To stand by or adhere to that which has been decided. The common law doctrine of stare decisis attempts to give security and certainty to the law by following the policy that once a principle of law as applicable to a certain set of facts has been set forth in a decision, it forms a precedent which will subsequently be followed, even though a different decision might be made were it the first time the question had arisen. Of course, stare decisis is not an inviolable principle and is departed from in instances where there is good cause (e.g., considerations of public policy led the Supreme Court to disregard prior decisions sanctioning segregation).

SUPRA: Above. A word referring a reader to an earlier part of a book.

ULTRA VIRES: Beyond the power. This phrase is most commonly used to refer to actions taken by a corporation that are beyond the power or legal authority of the corporation.

ADDENDUM OF FRENCH DERIVATIVES

IN PAIS: Not pursuant to legal proceedings.

CHATTEL: Tangible personal property.

CY PRES: Doctrine permitting courts to apply trust funds to purposes not expressed in the trust but necessary to carry out the settlor's intent.

PER AUTRE VIE: For another's life; in property law, an estate may be granted that will terminate upon the death of someone other than the grantee.

PROFIT A PRENDRE: A license to remove minerals or other produce from land.

VOIR DIRE: Process of questioning jurors as to their predispositions about the case or parties to a proceeding in order to identify those jurors displaying bias or prejudice.

REV 1-95

CASENOTE LEGAL BRIEFS

Administrative Law	Asimow, Bonfield & Levin
Administrative Law	Breyer, Stewart, Sunstein & Spitzer
Administrative Law	Cass, Diver & Beermann
Administrative Law	Funk, Shapiro & Weaver
Administrative Law	Reese
Administrative Law	Mashaw, Merrill & Shane
Administrative Law	Strauss, Rakoff & Farina (Gellhorn & Byse)
Agency & Partnership	Hynes & Loewenstein
Antitrust	Pitofsky, Goldschmid & Wood
Antitrust	Sullivan & Hovenkamp
Banking Law	Macey, Miller & Carnell
Bankruptcy	Warren & Bussel
Bankruptcy	Warren & Westbrook
Business Organizations	Eisenberg (Abridged & Unabridged)
Business Organizations	Choper, Coffee & Gilson
Business Organizations	Hamilton
Business Organizations	Klein, Ramseyer & Bainbridge
Business Organizations	O'Kelley & Thompson
Business Organizations	Soderquist, Sommer, Chew & Smiddy
Business Organizations	Bauman, Weiss & Palmiter
Civil Procedure	Cound, Friedenthal, Miller & Sexton
Civil Procedure	Field, Kaplan & Clermont
Civil Procedure	Freer & Perdue
Civil Procedure	Hazard, Tait & Fletcher
Civil Procedure	Marcus, Redish & Sherman
Civil Procedure	Subrin, Minow, Brodin & Main
Civil Procedure	Yeazell
Commercial Law	Jordan, Warren & Walt
Commercial Law	Lopucki, Warren, Keating & Mann
Commercial Law (Sales/Sec.Tr/Pay.Law)	Speidel, Summers & White
Commercial Law	Whaley
Community Property	Bird
Community Property	Blumberg
Complex Litigation	Marcus & Sherman
Conflicts	Brilmayer & Goldsmith
Conflicts	Currie, Kay & Kramer
Conflicts	Hay, Weintraub & Borchers
Conflicts	Symeonides, Perdue & Von Mehren
Constitutional Law	Brest, Levinson, Balkin & Amar
Constitutional Law	Chemerinsky
Constitutional Law	Choper, Fallon, Kamisar & Shiffrin (Lockhart)
Constitutional Law	Cohen & Varat
Constitutional Law	Farber, Eskridge & Frickey
Constitutional Law	Rotunda
Constitutional Law	Sullivan & Gunther
Constitutional Law	Stone, Seidman, Sunstein & Tushnet
Contracts	Barnett
Contracts	Burton
Contracts	Calamari, Perillo & Bender
Contracts	Crandall & Whaley
Contracts	Dawson, Harvey & Henderson
Contracts	Farnsworth, Young & Sanger
Contracts	Fuller & Eisenberg
Contracts	Knapp, Crystal & Prince
Contracts	Murphy, Speidel & Ayres
Contracts	Rosett & Bussel
Copyright	Goldstein
Copyright	Joyce, Leaffer, Jaszi & Ochoa
Criminal Law	Bonnie, Coughlin, Jeffries & Low
Criminal Law	Boyce & Perkins
Criminal Law	Johnson & Cloud
Criminal Law	Kadish & Schulhofer
Criminal Law	Kaplan, Weisberg & Binder
Criminal Procedure	Allen, Stuntz, Hoffmann & Livingston
Criminal Procedure	Dressler & Thomas
Criminal Procedure	Haddad, Marsh, Zagel, Meyer, Starkman & Bauer
Criminal Procedure	Kamisar, La Fave, Israel & King
Criminal Procedure	Saltzburg & Capra
Criminal Procedure	Weaver, Abramson, Bacigal, Burkhoff, Hancock & Lively
Criminal Procedure	Weinreb
Employment Discrimination	Friedman & Strickler
Employment Discrimination	Zimmer, Sullivan, Richards & Calloway
Employment Law	Rothstein & Liebman
Environmental Law	Menell & Stewart
Environmental Law	Percival, Miller, Schroder & Leape
Environmental Law	Plater, Abrams, Goldfarb & Graham
Evidence	Broun, Mosteller & Giannelli
Evidence	Mueller & Kirkpatrick
Evidence	Sklansky
Evidence	Waltz & Park
Evidence	Weinstein, Mansfield, Abrams & Berger
Evidence	Wellborn
Family Law	Areen
Family Law	Ellman, Kurtz & Scott
Family Law	Harris & Teitelbaum
Family Law	Krause, Oldham, Elrod & Garrison
Family Law	Wadlington & O'Brien
Family Law	Weisberg & Appleton
Federal Courts	Fallon, Meltzer & Shapiro (Hart & Wechsler)
Federal Courts	Low & Jeffries
Federal Courts	Redish & Sherry
First Amendment	Shiffrin & Choper
Gender and Law	Bartlett & Harris
Health Care Law	Hall, Bobinski & Orentlicher
Health Law	Furrow, Greaney, Johnson, Jost & Schwartz
Immigration Law	Aleinikoff, Martin & Motomura
Immigration Law	Legomsky
Indian Law	Getches, Wilkinson & Williams
Insurance Law	Abraham
Intellectual Property	Merges, Menell & Lemley
International Business Transactions	Folsom, Gordon & Spanogle
International Law	Carter & Trimble
International Law	Damrosch, Henkin, Pugh, Schachter & Smit
International Law	Dunoff, Ratner & Wippman
International Law	Firmage, Blakesley, Scott & Williams (Sweeny & Oliver)
Labor Law	Cox, Bok, Gorman & Finkin
Land Use	Callies, Freilich & Roberts
Legislation	Eskridge, Frickey & Garrett
Mass Media	Franklin, Anderson & Cate
Oil & Gas	Kuntz, Lowe, Anderson, Smith & Pierce
Patent Law	Adelman, Radner, Thomas & Wegner
Patent Law	Francis & Collins
Products Liability	Owen, Montgomery & Keeton
Professional Responsibility	Gillers
Professional Responsibility	Hazard, Koniak & Cramton
Professional Responsibility	Morgan & Rotunda
Professional Responsibility	Schwartz, Wydick & Perschbacher
Property	Casner, Leach, French, Korngold & Vandervelde
Property	Cribbet, Johnson, Findley & Smith
Property	Donahue, Kauper & Martin
Property	Dukeminier & Krier
Property	Haar & Liebman
Property	Kurtz & Hovenkamp
Property	Nelson, Stoebuck & Whitman
Property	Rabin, Kwall & Kwall
Property	Singer
Real Estate	Berger & Johnstone
Real Estate	Korngold & Goldstein
Real Estate Transactions	Nelson & Whitman
Remedies	Rendleman (Bauman & York)
Remedies	Laycock
Remedies	Leavell, Love, Nelson & Kovacic-Fleisher
Remedies	Re & Re
Remedies	Shoben, Tabb & Janutis
Securities Regulation	Cox, Hillman & Langevoort
Securities Regulation	Jennings, Marsh & Coffee
Software and Internet Law	Lemley, Menell, Merges & Samuelson
Sports Law	Weiler & Roberts
Sports Law	Yasser, McCurdy, Goplerud & Weston
Taxation (Corporate)	Lind, Schwartz, Lathrope & Rosenberg
Taxation (Estate & Gift)	Bittker, Clark & McCouch
Taxation (Individual)	Burke & Friel
Taxation (Individual)	Freeland, Lind, Stephens & Lathrope
Taxation (Individual)	Graetz & Schenk
Taxation (Individual)	Klein, Bankman & Shaviro
Torts	Dobbs & Hayden
Torts	Epstein
Torts	Franklin & Rabin
Torts	Henderson, Pearson & Siliciano
Torts	Wade, Schwartz, Kelly & Partlett (Prosser)
Wills, Trusts, & Estates	Dukeminier & Johanson
Wills, Trusts, & Estates	Ritchie, Alford & Effland (Dobris & Sterk)
Wills, Trusts, & Estates	Scoles, Halbach, Link & Roberts
Wills, Trusts, & Estates	Waggoner, Alexander, Fellows & Gallanis